EFFECTIVE PRINCIPALS

POSITIVE PRINCIPLES AT WORK

James O'Hanlon
Donald O. Clifton

ScarecrowEducation
Lanham, Maryland • Toronto • Oxford
2004

Published in the United States of America
by ScarecrowEducation
An imprint of The Rowman & Littlefield Publishing Group, Inc.
4501 Forbes Boulevard, Suite 200, Lanham, Maryland 20706
www.scarecroweducation.com

PO Box 317
Oxford
OX2 9RU, UK

British Library Cataloguing in Publication Information Available

Library of Congress Cataloging-in-Publication Data

O'Hanlon, James, 1936–
 Effective principals : positive principles at work / James O'Hanlon, Donald
O. Clifton.
  p. cm.
 Includes bibliographical references.
 ISBN 1-57886-132-2 (pbk. : alk. paper)
 ISBN: 978-1-57886-132-3

 1. School principals—Professional relationships. 2. Educational
leadership. I. Clifton, Donald O. II. Title.
 LB2831.9.O53 2004
 371.2'012—dc22

2004000087

♾™ The paper used in this publication meets the minimum requirements of
American National Standard for Information Sciences—Permanence of Paper for
Printed Library Materials, ANSI/NISO Z39.48-1992.
Manufactured in the United States of America.

CONTENTS

PREFACE

"I started twelve years ago. When I go out in the community I see so many people who were once kids in our school. They all want to talk with me. They let you know that you touched them in a positive way. This is probably the most noble of all the professions because we are helping people in all kinds of ways."
—*a California high school principal*

For many years, the Gallup Organization has been conducting research that has documented the critical importance of leadership to the success of organizations of all kinds. In business, it has been found that the manager is the key to the success of the organization. Indicators of customer satisfaction, profitability, employee satisfaction, and staying with the organization are among those outcomes highly affected by the quality of the work of the manager.[1] Similar results are found for leaders in government and other settings. Managers are at the center of organizational success.

Gallup's studies of effective managers have identified that they are adherents to the tenets of "positive psychology" in their work as managers. Whether they recognize it or not, this is the basis for their actions and for their success.

Positive psychology involves these principles:

- Building on success gets greater return on investment than working to eliminate failure.
- Building works better than fixing.

- Basing your work on a concept of the "good life" leads to success.
- Investing in others makes you feel good.
- Responding to positivity is more natural for people than responding to negativity.
- Working to broaden and build people leads them to have more and better ideas.
- Building positive emotions in the organization broadens and builds personal resources of the organization's members.[2]

We undertook the study reported here to determine if school principals are also key to the success of their schools as leaders and managers are in other professions. They are. What we found about the work of principals rated as outstanding was most impressive. Like successful business managers they too implement "positive psychology" in their work. They do this in a consistent way. Their feelings are well integrated, which allows them to respond effectively to the feelings of those with whom they work. They present a positive, dependable model for the others in their schools.

These outstanding principals have a powerful effect on their schools as well as on the individuals in them, both students and staff. Their influence is an affirmative one for many. They help others have better lives. Truly their work is that of a noble profession. Their work is of singular importance to their schools. There are many good principals in the schools of this country. Those effective principals who exhibit the principles of positive psychology in their everyday work, however, bring their schools something extra that produces greater growth for all involved. They apply positive psychology to the benefit of those with whom they work. These principals are a group apart. They are unusually effective leaders.

To carry out this study we conducted a series of focus group interviews of principals identified as excellent by those who prepare principals and provide them continuing education in California, Nebraska, Illinois, New Jersey, Virginia, and Alabama. In addition experienced telephone interviewers from the Gallup Organization interviewed a sample of principals who had been selected as Principals of the Year in their states over a two-year period by state affiliates of the National Association of Elementary School Principals and the National Association of Secondary School Principals. Both of these sources yielded substantial data about highly effective principals. To verify the selection of these principals as outstanding we did two things. We surveyed teachers in the schools of a sample of this group to determine if they, too, would describe these principals as outstanding, and we compared what we had learned from the principals in our study with a sample of all principals in our state (Nebraska) to determine if there were real differences in how they worked. Both of these approaches documented that the principals we studied were in fact a special group.

In our study we talked with principals from urban high schools with as many as 3,500 students and from rural schools with just more than 100 students enrolled. Regardless of the size of the school, type of school, grade level, or location we found these effective principals to have much in common. What they told us about their work, how they do it, and why they do it was surprisingly consistent. We had expected to find marked differences between elementary and secondary principals, principals in different states, and principals in schools of different sizes. Although the specific tasks of their jobs vary, school principals all share the common responsibility of leading a school and making it strong. How the best principals do this is remarkably constant.

These principals are passionate about their work. Whether in the focus-group setting or the telephone interview, they talked readily about what they do. They enjoyed the opportunity to talk about their work. It was difficult to bring the focus group sessions or the telephone interviews to a close because they wanted to continue to talk. A number of principals drove long distances to participate in the focus groups and then thanked us for the opportunity to do so. They were really fun groups to interview. It did not take much to get them to talk enthusiastically about their schools. It's no surprise that these leaders dedicate an exceptional number of hours per week to their jobs. They love their work.

The chapters ahead will describe the work of those principals who apply positive psychology to their profession and how they maintain their dedication to their work. You will see why we view their work as being such a noble profession and why you should too.

In writing about these principals we have chosen to use the pronoun "she," although obviously not all of them are female. In fact most principals are male. On the elementary level the split between males and females in the principalship is fairly even, but on the secondary level females are clearly in the minority. Alternating "she" and "he" in our writing was a possibility but a little messy. Using something like she/he seemed especially awkward. Perhaps the English language needs a new pronoun besides the impersonal "it" to refer to either males or females. In the end we decided to use "she" because we hope that this might in some way encourage more women to consider becoming principals. Interestingly, the outstanding principals group we studied included a higher percentage of females than the control group of principals we compared them with. With the developing shortage of people preparing to be principals, perhaps one way to deal with this is to attract more females to the field.

We hope for several outcomes from this study:

- We hope that the public will better understand the incredibly demanding nature of the principal's job.
- We want to help provide recognition to principals for the significant leadership they provide.
- We hope that parents will appreciate the importance of the principal to the quality of their children's education.
- We want to encourage parents to expect that the schools their children attend will have highly capable principals. We want also to encourage them to provide strong support to such principals to enable them to fully exercise their leadership.
- We hope also that this study will encourage highly able individuals to become principals. Learning about the enthusiasm that these effective principals have for their work and the great dedication they exhibit may lead individuals with similar qualities to the profession of principalship.

We believe that the information in this book will help prospective principals determine whether it is the career for them—and this job is a career, a profession in itself. Most of the principals we studied do not view their position as a stepping stone to some other kind of work. They expect to remain principals until they retire.

Finally we hope that the reader will find these outstanding principals to be as fascinating as we did in talking with them. We have included many of their statements so you can get to know them better. They are truly special people, and the students, staff, and communities of their schools are fortunate to work with them. What follows is the story of those effective principals we found who implement positive principles in their work and the wonderful results they accomplish.

NOTES

1. J. K. Harter, F. L. Schmidt, and E. A. Killham, *Employment Engagement, Satisfaction, and Business-Unit-Level Outcomes: A Meta-Analysis.* (Washington, D.C.: The Gallup Organization, 2003).

2. B. L. Fredrickson, "The Role of Positive Emotions in Positive Psychology: The Broaden-and-Build Theory of Positive Emotions," *American Psychologist* 56 (2001): 218–26.

1

DOES IT MAKE A DIFFERENCE?

Does it make a difference who the principal of your child's school is? Obviously it takes many people—teachers, staff, students, and community members—to provide a good school for your child to attend. It takes adequate resources—a good facility, up-to-date instructional materials, instructional equipment—as well. Fortunately most schools have dedicated principals to lead them. The October 2001 Gallup National Principalship Survey indicated that only 5 percent of those polled had a negative opinion of the principal. That survey also indicated that 85 percent believed that the principal was either "extremely important" or "very important" to their school.

So most people are satisfied with the leadership of the schools their children are attending and the results these schools are getting. That's great news. The question that intrigued us, however, is whether it is possible that schools with outstanding leadership can do even better. Is leadership the critical element in the level of success a school achieves? Are schools led by outstanding principals—those principals we found—identifiably different from schools in general? Is there a better environment that produces growth in students and staff alike? Is there more academic growth? Is there more social growth? Our study indicates that schools in which these effective principals work are indeed special.

WHAT IS THE EFFECTIVE PRINCIPAL'S
EFFECT ON ACADEMIC GROWTH?

"Two years after Saratoga school got a new principal achievement scores in reading and math were up by as much as 20 percent. Disciplinary problems had decreased and parent and community involvement in the school increased. One parent observed, 'He has a vision. It's kind of like he has this little train and people want to get on board.'"[1] "Under the leadership of a strong principal, Elliott elementary school saw improvements of 10 percent in reading and 14 percent in math scores. Disciplinary referrals fell by 80 percent. A parent commented that she has never known a school that cares so much about kids."[2]

Effective principals support high student achievement. How does this happen?

1. They set high expectations for the work of students and faculty. They get students and faculty to buy into these expectations and to embrace them for themselves.
2. They establish an environment that enables all to focus on academic work.
3. They marshal the resources of the school to focus them on academic performance. They encourage and challenge, encourage and challenge.
4. They recognize and salute progress. Their intense desire to succeed rubs off on those with whom they work.
5. They persist.

DOES THE POSITIVE PRINCIPAL
INFLUENCE SCHOOL CLIMATE?

The positive principal's work and style creates an atmosphere that is conducive to growth. She conveys spirit and energy to the staff, students, and community. Teachers experience such principals as being compassionate, loving, and caring, but also as holding high expectations for student and staff performance as well as for her own performance. A culture of high expectation, of striving for excellence, is created.

What the effective principal believes about the people with whom she works is probably how they will perform. If she believes that the staff will be successful and that the students in the school will be successful, both will rise to those expectations. The principal is a very powerful human being in the school setting. She is the focal point and the driving force behind much of what happens in the school. The principal can make or break a school through the environment she creates.

The climate of the school is in many ways an extension of the principal's personality. It takes on the feeling, tone, and appeal. One principal in our study humorously stated this strong effect this way: "I think that I have heard that some schools even smell like the principal because as the principal walks from room to room that fragrance, whatever kind of fragrance that the lady wears, follows her along."

HOW DOES THE EFFECTIVE PRINCIPAL SHAPE THE SCHOOL?

When students and staff see the principal giving her best every day, they strive to do so also. When students and staff see the principal having fun and enjoying herself, they enjoy themselves in their work as well. She creates an environment of success.

Those in the school look to the principal for what is appropriate behavior. For the principal it's like being on stage all the time. Others react to her reactions so it is important that she is always positive. In tense situations the principal needs to be cool, calm, and collected or things will become chaotic and negative. It's as if the principal's behavior is catching. This is especially true in situations where order is required. The principal's presence has a strong impact on maintaining order. The principal's behavior establishes a sense of integrity for the school and demonstrates how conflict can be managed positively.

Part of the tone setting by the principal is the principal's work ethic. Effective principals never ask their staffs to do or complete any task they would not take on themselves. If the floors are messed up and water is coming in everywhere from a broken pipe, the odds are that the principal will be one of the persons with a mop cleaning up. The principal sets the example.

The tone of the school is also set through the principal's model of positive behavior. As one principal in our study stated, "You've got to walk the talk constantly, so you've got to be peppy, you've got to be smiley, you've got to be happy, and I mean your voice tone has to always be on the positive. You've got to smile, you've got to smile." The compassion that the principal shows for those with whom she works is then reflected in how the rest of the staff works with students. The principal's enthusiasm is contagious and soon becomes the tone of the school.

You really need an effective principal for your school because such a principal helps others be more successful. Effective principals apply the tenets of positive psychology in their work. They build on success, respond to positive actions, and invest in others. They have a strong belief about what their schools can be. They focus on building positive emotions in their organizations.

The effective principal creates an atmosphere in which students and staff can flourish. She develops a structure that enables people to use their best talents. She enables all to have a voice in what happens in the school. The effective principal's goal is not to become the star but to make other people the star. As a teacher said about one of the principals in our study, "She enables others to shine for whatever is always best for our children and their families. She has a servant's attitude and treats every one in our building like royalty."

The effective principal is like the quarterback of a football team. She pulls together a staff that is unified on where it is going and committed to the highest performance. Outstanding schools have effective principals. Effective principals develop outstanding schools. Although principals are often unsung heroes in their communities they are truly part of the nobility of any community. You want a principal who practices positive psychology for your school.

NOTES

1. "Saratoga Nominated for National School Award," *Lincoln Journal-Star*, 12 January 2001.

2. "Elliott Turns the Corner," *Lincoln Journal-Star*, 16 December 2001.

2

WHAT'S THE DAY OF A PRINCIPAL LIKE?

It is not possible to give a very definite answer to the question "What's the day of the principal like?" That's because every day is different, new, and unpredictable in many ways. Here's what a day might look like:

A DAY FROM AN ELEMENTARY PRINCIPAL'S JOURNAL

7:20 Arrive. Turn on computers, make coffee, check e-mail.

7:25 Call from kitchen.

7:27 Call from a parent who wants to explore the possibility of getting her son assigned to a behavior-disordered room for the remainder of the year. He has been suspended several times, and she doesn't think a regular school is the right placement for him. I explained the process of getting a child assigned to such a room, and reiterated the interventions we were implementing with Walter. We discussed Rule 51, his 504 plan, and his specific behaviors. She was complimentary about what we were doing. She agreed that the interventions should be given more time to work. We agreed to have an IEP meeting in late January to review progress.

7:40 Student arrives early. Placed her in lobby until breakfast (8:15).

7:45 Teacher requests conference about upset parent. We discussed what teacher should have done (walk student to nurse, show concern about braid being pulled out, gather facts, let office know of problem, write referral if warranted). Followed up with phone call to parent. Parent still upset, requested conference with teacher at 8:30.

7:57 Phone call, parent reporting child absence.

8:15 SAT (student assistance team meeting), Room 13, leave early to attend 8:30 meeting.

8:30 Meeting with parent about braid issue, in office, mother upset, loud voice, crying because daughter had braid "pulled out by boy, nobody cared, teacher didn't even look at head, sent daughter to nurse, didn't send anyone to walk with her, nobody called to #911 or to mom when it happened, etc." Teacher told mother it was accidental according to other student accounts, that she did look at the head, and the counselor intercepted the child and walked her to the nurse. Mother said it was on purpose and she should have an apology, she was going to press charges against the little boy. I sympathized with mother, told her we would look into the situation and get back to her. She left less upset.

8:48 John called about my request for Sudanese psychiatrist or therapist to assist with ESL student with limited English and severe behavioral issues, resulting in aggression and anger outbursts. He said he will get Medicaid to assist, and would find help. Will have answer before end of day tomorrow.

8:50 Assist with student monitoring in breakfast and auditorium.

8:55 Monitor student dismissal from breakfast and auditorium going to classrooms. Visited first- and fourth-grade rooms.

9:05 Referrals on three students; fight before entering room. Assigned consequences. Called for three boys who were rough-housing after school on school grounds yesterday. Discussed reasons why that's not allowed. Natural consequences: Wait in auditorium for bus, instead of waiting outside.

9:30 Questioned Frank about braid incident. He mentioned two other girls who saw incident. Called them in; interviewed girls. They corroborated Frank's story. Wrote incident report. Called Dara's mother to give her the girls' accounts. She was not receptive, still believing it was done on purpose. Left message for Frank's mother to call. Spoke with nurse, asked why she did not call mother to tell of braid incident. She apologized and said she'd call mom.

9:33 Note from Resource teacher: Case worker for Timmy can't make it to IEP. Asked if we should reschedule for one person. As I was writing note to her, got a call from Special Education supervisor, who said she couldn't make it to the IEP and if we want to change his placement, she has to be there. I scheduled another date and time, called foster mom and case worker and told them new time. Finished note to Special Education teacher, and asked for proof if student's mom has parental rights intact.

10:00 Visited sixth-grade rooms, computer lab, library, ESL room. Good-morning rounds.

10:35 Parent call requesting step-child visiting for vacation be allowed to spend next day at school with brother. Kindly explained why that isn't possible and thanked her for being so understanding.

10:45 Referral to office for Paul masturbating in class. Met with him; he denied doing so, even though there were three written accounts from students sitting near him who witnessed the event. Father was called. No answer. Left message for dad to call.

11:00 Met with teacher and counselor about Paul. We're perplexed, as he takes no responsibility for any of his actions, no matter how trivial. Counselor took Paul for some "counseling."

11:15 Signed reports for sub desk and payroll, as we talked about Paul.

11:30-1:10 Cafeteria. Two referrals arrived in cafeteria. Asked Security to have secretary call one student's home and have mom come—sent him home for rest of day. (Severe disruption and disrespect.) Samantha's mother said she was on the way.

1:15 Met with Samantha's mom. Started off defensive, but came around. Decided on 1.5 day suspension, and a meeting with teacher day after suspension. Stressed to mom that Samantha needs to see us as a team, not as adversaries, which has been the case. She admitted that she does get defensive.

2:00 Ate lunch and interviewed three first-graders who fought on playground. Assigned consequences and sent home form letter to all parents. Same time, sister of security guard (Margaret) came, didn't know he had not reported for work. Told her what I knew. (Birthday yesterday. Was going to celebrate, may have over-celebrated, did not report for work and did not call in, and we couldn't reach him by phone.)

2:10 Margaret called, Tom not answering door or phone. Worried. Told her I'd call around to other people who know him. Made call to Mary, who started to call others.

2:30 Opened school mail. Gave Martin Luther King essay contest fliers to secretary to distribute. Margaret and Mary both called about Tom.

2:35 Conferred with assistant principal about suspension case, student hitting teacher. Agreed on three-day, and reassignment to another room upon his return. Tried to contact mother. No phone. Wrote letter. Another call from Margaret; still no Tom. Mary called. No luck. We're worried now.

3:00 Police arrived to interview student about marks on arm. Took them to the counselor's office.

3:05 Middle school counselor called to offer us five food baskets. Must get names of families, address, phone, etc., to them TOMORROW, and families have to be at home Sat. between 8:30 and 10:30 am to receive. Involved counselors, who took over.

3:10 Tom called. He was sleeping. Couldn't hear phone. Told him to call his mother, and I'll get him big time tomorrow.

3:15 Call from parent wanting child to be released early and allowed to walk home. Gave ok if child or mom will call as soon as he arrives.

3:27 Neighbor of school called to complain about trash. Suggested that fifth-graders go around and pick it up every day. I wanted to tell her what she could do, but instead I told her we'd take care of it. Put a note in head engineer's box that trash was causing neighbor problems and would he please see to it. I looked out and saw one plastic bag floating in the air. No other trash visible from my window.

3:30 Human Resources called about personnel issue. Bad news. Employee has to be terminated due to felony conviction.

3:40 Dismissal bell. Outside with radio.

4:20 Come in from dismissal. Nine students still not picked up. Start them calling their parents/rides.

4:22 ESL supervisor calls. We decide to move Carol from fourth to fifth grade. Talked about John getting us help with therapist or psychiatrist. Also touched base on para resigning and need for immediate replacement. Told Susan I'd call HR and see what the possibilities are.

4:30 Called HR, talked to Jim about replacing ESL para. He said postings out.

4:40 Started to clear off table and desk. Phone call from parent looking for child. As we were talking, child got home.

4:45 Students from cheerleading came in. No one has picked them up. Made phone calls home. Waited for rides to arrive. Checked e-mail. Answered e-mail.

5:00 Mother called, crying because her daughter was being picked on by other girls. Wants Madeline put in another room. I asked if Madeline was telling the teacher when girls picked on her. No. Told her we would have to try to stop the bullying problem, and that moving Madeline might be the answer, but we'd have to do a little exploring. Mother agreed. Will call girls to office first thing tomorrow.

5:20 Paul's father called. I explained the allegations of masturbation or at the least, inappropriate behavior. Read to him the accounts from student witnesses. We discussed the pattern of behavior we are both seeing (no ownership of behavior; lying) and discussed what to do. Both of us perplexed at this point.

5:45 Started to clean desk. ESL teacher brought in requisition for textbooks and supplies. I coded requisition and placed in school mail. We visited about Carol, and moving a para to first grade and kindergarten.

6:00 Phone call for teacher. Already left.

6:15 Left for the day.

It's obvious from following this principal's day that she becomes involved in many human relations situations that need a steady hand. She is called upon to respond quickly and in ways that will head the situation toward a positive resolution. This requires a well-internalized philosophy about what she is doing and a developmental approach to working with people. It is also clear that one quality the principal must have is the "executive abandon" capacity. She must be able to switch from one topic, situation, or person to another rapidly, giving her full attention to the new claim on her time but remembering the old well enough that she follows up on it as necessary. Almost every situation with which she deals requires some kind of follow-up. She must be able to keep several "balls in the air" at one time and sometimes to engage in a conversation with more than one person at a time, making each feel that they have her attention. She is a true " multitasker."

ANOTHER ELEMENTARY SCHOOL PRINCIPAL'S DAY

7:30 Arrive and unpack the homework bag—a pile to file at a later date, stuff to put in staff boxes, responses to questions on notes, thank you's to staff who went above and beyond.

7:50 Upset mother calls to talk about her child needing to stay after school—threatens to take him out of school, go "to the Board," etc.

8:00 Quick look at calendar and e-mail.

8:10 Phone call from a UNTL collaborator.

8:15 Meet with a teacher who wants to "think with me" about her ideas, future plans, problems.

8:50 Greet students as they gather for the start of school.

9.00 School begins.

9:10 Children who are late to class stay in the office area and are released to classrooms in 10 minute increments—remind the children who are late to come earlier the next day.

9:15 Think Time with child.

(This morning—a child with behavior disorder is assigned to my office to complete the work he didn't complete the day before. He could not stay after school because of mom's work schedule and the teacher is working on a play and he demands so much attention that we worked out this plan.)

10:30 Meet with our Grant Facilitator to think about assessments and measuring the objectives in the grant.

11:00 Lunchroom duty.

11:30 Quick walk to get outside.

11:50 Return a phone call.

11:55 Observe a teacher.

1:00 Complete paperwork for District needs, look through mail, start packing my homework bag, make a couple calls, look at e-mail, talk with assistant principal. Talk with special education coordinator. (Some of these tasks happen at the same time.)

2:00 Meet with Community Learning Center people.

3:00 Continue with the work started at 1:00.

3:30 Greet parents on the benches in the hall.

3:38 Supervise dismissal.

4:00 Figure out who needs to call and find ways home.

4:10 Debrief with a Special Education paraprofessional who was bitten by a child with behavior disorders when he was out of control and the teacher had a substitute.

4:25 Meet with sixth-grade girls, their parents, teachers, school psychologist, and special education coordinator to discuss a plan for being inclusive and stopping the name calling, rumors, and troubles that start outside of school and spill over into school.

5:15 Return some calls, answer some e-mail.

5:30 Head home.

6:00 Family time.

9:30–11:30 Paperwork from school.

The principal who provided this log ended with this statement: "After I did this I realized that it really doesn't capture what the work is like—I don't see the excitement, challenge, complexity, and wonder that I experience and feel each day. I think it is the unique learning opportunities and the glimpses into multiple perspectives that make it such incredible work. The things I learn from are experiences like:

- working with translators to understand the school experiences of a child and his or her family who are new to America.
- learning from families the complexities of resources and support when financial resources are very limited. Hearing their voice.
- sitting at a table with NIFA, Neighborhood Inc., home builders, university faculty, bankers, city people, neighborhood association members, community agencies—thinking together about student mobility and stabilizing a neighborhood.
- thinking with collaborators about how to develop children who are peacemakers.
- working with university faculty on secondary interventions for children who are struggling as they learn to read.

- streaming funds to support school improvement.
- partnering with teachers as they talk and I try to understand the instructional decisions they made when I observed their lessons. Steering our conversation in a way that teachers continue to think about their instruction.
- thinking and studying the data to determine activities for School Improvement as a learning organization.
- building partners throughout the community."

ONE HIGH SCHOOL PRINCIPAL'S DAY

6:45 Arrive at building. Try to finish reading e-mails that arrived yesterday. Many of the e-mails protest the decision to cancel a school dance scheduled for next week due to lack of organization by the sponsoring student group. Phone rings three times before the office is officially open with information and questions from parents.

7:00 Stand outside office and talk with teachers as they arrive. One wants to talk about a problem with a student—I promise to visit her class today or tomorrow to observe the student; another about a curriculum issue; a third wants to continue a discussion started yesterday about difficulties a younger teacher is having and how to help him. A fourth wants to tell me about the elementary school play her child was in last night, a fifth about how her ill mother is doing.

7:30 Meet with School Foundation Board about an upcoming fund raising project. Make a note to check back in a couple of days with the chair of the project to make certain people are being contacted.

8:15 Meet with cheerleader sponsors about the upcoming selection of new cheerleaders. Trying to find a way to make this event less traumatic for those not chosen. Will meet again in a week.

8:40 Walk through the building. Visit three classes during walk through, including class of the teacher from the earlier conversation. Interrupted by assistant principal who notifies me that he must take a student who is ill to the hospital; school secretary is trying to contact the parents.

10:00 Meet with two students who were in a fight in the school parking lot. Secure apologies and talk about how to keep this kind of situation from happening. Remind students that next such episode will result in suspension.

10:30 Meet with school counselor about problems some new students in the school are encountering. Counselor has an idea about a student mentor program that she wants to develop.

11:00 Return phone calls that have come in during the morning (six from parents with a variety of concerns about their students, one from the police about the possibility that they may have to come to school to arrest a student, one from superintendent's office with questions about our requests for some additional computer equipment, one from Foundation Board member who does not like part of the plan agreed to at the meeting this morning, one from principal at another school who wants to know what our experience is with some curriculum materials).

11:30 Lunch supervision; grab some lunch at a table with some students. Take advantage of the time in the lunchroom to talk with the student the teacher had expressed concern about earlier.

12:30 Job target planning with assistant principal; interrupted by custodian who states one of the main doors is broken—assistant principal will redesign exit routes for students to get to buses today.

1:15 Go out in halls between classes; looking for two students who have serious illnesses in their families to see how they are doing. Also talked with teacher about how student who had been put on threat of suspension was doing in his class now.

1:25 Conference with teacher concerning plans for science fair and support she needs for that. This is our third meeting about this and plans now appear ready. Need to alert custodians to this event.

1:40 Return phone calls (two from parents each of whom wants their student to have excused absences for a family trip, one from community member about problem created by students leaving school who stop to smoke on a corner near her house).

1:55 Meet with Student Council president about plans for upcoming meeting. President really is not prepared; plan to meet again tomorrow.

2:15 Walk through school. Talk with two teachers during their planning periods about issues they have with students and the librarian about a complaint received from a community member about a book. Talk briefly with the teacher who expressed concern about a student this morning; we plan to meet later this week to talk about a plan for improving the student's performance.

2:40 Return to office and three students are waiting, each with a different problem.

3:15 Go out in halls for school dismissal; oversee school bus loading.

3:45 Meet with staff development committee concerning plans for next fall. We each agree to talk with four teachers about their ideas before going any further.

4:00 Meeting with Mr. Smith about the field trip he is planning for his biology class. Since he is a new teacher and has not taken a field trip before we talked about kinds of permissions and arrangements that will be needed.

4:25 Meeting with Ms. Johnson about how to handle a feud between two students in her class.

5:00 School secretary goes over issues that have come up during the day.

5:15 Start on paperwork. Work on agenda for faculty meeting in two days. Also on student discipline/due process records which take a lot of time.

5:45 Calls to get two substitute teachers for the next day.

6:00 Start responding to e-mails which have come in during the day.

6:30 Grab a quick sandwich at nearby fast food restaurant.

7:00 Meet with Parent Advisory Council. After meeting one parent wants to talk about issues her student has with a coach.

8:30 Head for home.

In some ways it appears that the principal is like the head of a family. A wide range of problems is brought to her. People seek her opinion on many issues. She is alert to personal problems people in the school are having and provides support to them. Those in the school, students and staff, want to involve her in what they are doing.

Most principals will tell you that there are no two days alike. It is good to plan for the day as long as you don't become tied to carrying out the plan. If the principal does not do some planning, and especially some reflecting on what is happening, she will be unprepared for the day, for things are going to happen fast. But regardless of how much planning is done the day will take its own course (e.g., one principal reported that she had to delay the school schedule one day because she did not want students passing to classrooms in other buildings during a lightning storm). The principal's schedule is made for her by events and by others. Trying to do something as routine as scheduling a dentist appointment becomes a complicated task for the principal. Most likely the appointment will have to be changed several times because of things that come up. The leader principal truly learns to "go with the flow."

WHEN IS THE PRINCIPAL ON DUTY?

Perhaps someone who views the work of the principal from a distance would think that she shows up shortly before school and leaves for the day after the students leave. And that she has her summers off to vacation and spend time with her family and hobbies. In reality the work of an effective principal is about as far from that description as it could get. It's closer to being a 365 day a year, 24 hour a day job than a job that only happens when students are in classes. The principal is like an actress who never gets off stage. Wherever she goes in the community she is the principal. Few jobs have a pace that rivals that of a principal. Principals are never off duty. It's an awesome responsibility. And they love it.

The principal is on call 24 hours a day, 365 days a year. Her life is controlled by the school calendar. When she is not on the job she is processing what's going on at school. When she goes home at night her mind is still going with things from the day. It's hard to ever turn off. As one principal said, "Some of my best solutions come from sitting on the garage floor fixing my mower." Everything the effective principal does revolves around the job. Two principals in this study who are married to each other joke about talking about their work even when they are brushing their teeth. When the effective principal is on vacation she is looking for books that her teachers might like or materials for students to use or thinking about ideas to bring back to her staff.

Summers are not the time off for the principal that many might think. There are teachers to be hired, summer programs to direct, winding up the last school year, and preparing for the next. It's also a time that students, past and present, and teachers stop in for long visits about matters important to them. Even the principal's planned summer vacation may be disrupted by a call from the school. "I was on vacation in another state when I got a call from my superintendent that one of our teachers had unexpectedly accepted a job in another district. Since this was the end of July and not long before the start of school I had to cut my vacation short to come back to recruit another teacher before the August board meeting so he or she could be appointed to start the year."

The principal is on call regardless of where she is because "they" are going to find her. One principal said that she could be in Fiji and they will find her. "They" is everybody. Students, teachers, parents, community members, local officials, the superintendent, board of education members, and more. "When I go to school on the weekend to catch up on paperwork I have to hide my car or I will begin to get calls and have people drop in to see me." If there is something that affects the school the principal will be contacted.

"Two nights last week I was called, once at 11:30 and the other time at 1:00 in the morning, and I had to go to the school. When they call and say this is the police department I know I have to go." What might lead to a call to the principal late at night at her home? A school neighbor calls to say the school bells are ringing constantly; there has been an electrical malfunction. A student has been critically injured in a car accident. A custodian is seriously depressed and wants the principal's help in getting admitted to a hospital. A faculty member is drunk and wants the principal to give him a ride home. There has been a break-in at the school. There are lots of situations which may extend the principal's workday well after she has gone home.

The principal is on the job wherever she goes in the community. If she is grocery shopping it's likely that a parent, current student, or former student will want to talk with her about a school matter. Some find they have to do their grocery shopping out of their school area if they are to get it done in a reasonable period of time. If she goes out to eat the same thing happens.

One middle-level principal who is involved in scouting finds that people want to talk with her about school issues when she is at a scout meeting. Another who likes to attend high school athletic contests to watch former students play finds herself cornered by parents who want to talk for thirty minutes about the future of instrumental music in the schools or some other such subject important to them. As a result she misses a good part of the game she came to watch.

These conversations, while they interrupt the principal's "personal time," are often very valuable. They are clearly important to those who want to talk to the principal. It may be about something that the person is hesitant to bring up at school. Comments from former students are often very rewarding, for they frequently want to tell the principal about how much their school experience did for them. The principal is a high visibility person in her community, in and out of school.

WHAT DOES THE PRINCIPAL DO ALL DAY LONG?

Most principals arrive at school very early, perhaps as early as 6:30 a.m. Their day may start before they leave home with a call about a problem with the school building or the need to secure a substitute because a teacher is ill. If not, the day starts as soon as they hit the parking lot because someone is likely to be there waiting for them with a problem or an issue for their attention.

Much important work is done early in the morning. For some principals it is the chance to get things prepared for the day. For many it is the opportunity to have conversations with staff and students as they enter the building. This sends a message to staff and students alike that they are going to be supported during that day. In smaller schools leader principals try to greet each student at the beginning of the day. This helps establish a positive school climate.

Having a late day is not uncommon for the high school principal. "School's out for the day but I am triple-booked for after school. I have a soccer tournament, a softball tournament, and a varsity baseball game. So I make an appearance at the soccer tournament, I make an appearance at the softball tournament, I have an appearance at the varsity baseball game and at 9:30 that evening I go home."

The day involves conversations with many people, decisions to make, problems to solve. Despite good planning the principal does not know what the day will bring. What some call the "ambush factor" is especially demanding. Situations will come up unexpectedly and involve difficult decisions to be made quickly. Having to deal with an unusual situation that requires a decision in thirty seconds—that's what breeds mistakes, but it often cannot be avoided. One thing is for certain. Effective principals never get bored.

Problem solving, mediating, advising, encouraging, recommending—these are the principal's frequent activities. In many ways the principal's job is one of crisis management. Dealing with many situations in a way that maintains the educational environment of the school and supports teacher and student performance—that's the daily challenge for the principal. While one might think of the principal's job as dealing with students, it's often adults who take the most time and bring the most problems. Sometimes an event, such as the death of a student, will happen and totally consume the school. The principal's leadership is critical at this point. How she reacts greatly affects how others deal with the situation.

The principal cannot be a person who has a high need for closure because that's often not possible. The principal must be flexible, but flexible within a set of clear parameters. Many problems and situations need time to resolve—and frequently require many conversations. The principal is always teaching and modeling in every interaction in which she is involved. One principal described what all strong principals experience in this way:

"People who are not principals will stand off and watch all of us and after like fifteen minutes they will say you know you talked about fifteen different things in this very short period of time and you shifted gears very quickly. If you can't do that you are in trouble in this job."

During the day effective principals spend little time in their offices. Like top managers and leaders in other fields they are away from their offices, in the school and the community, almost three-fourths of the time. When the principal is not at school for some reason, everyone—students, staff, parents—notices. They want the principal to be visible . . . and the principal wants to be.

A highlight of the day for many principals is visiting classes and seeing teachers and students at work. This recharges the principal's "batteries." It's a real treat for the principal to watch the many wonderful things that teachers and students do every hour of the day. They especially enjoy visiting a class where their presence does not interrupt anything. "When you walk into a classroom and nothing stops, the kids are all engaged and it's difficult to find the teacher among them and they don't realize you are there—I really like that."

Effective principals want to be out in the school, with the students and the staff. One cannot be a leader by sitting in one's office for much of the day. The principal has to be involved. This is how the principal finds out what is going on so she can determine what issues need to be addressed. Students and staff alike who will not come to see the principal in her office will come up to the principal in the hall or the cafeteria or on the campus to visit about things important to them.

All kinds of situations come to the principal's attention as a result of being available through walking around the school. There's the teacher who confides in the principal that he is distraught about not being able to get in contact with his grown daughter. He fears she is being abused by her boyfriend. On hearing this the principal immediately drops everything else and goes looking for the daughter. Before the day is over she reports back to the teacher that she has talked with his daughter and she is okay and in no kind of trouble.

The effective principal's office becomes more of a stopping-off place rather than where a lot of the day's work is accomplished (with the exception of paperwork often done after 5:00 p.m., one of the principal's least favored parts of the job, and some private conferences). The principal views the office not as a personal refuge but as a school resource. An example of this is the principal in the school building constructed in 1930 where the lockers are too small to hold the new popular book bags on wheels many students have. The principal lets these students store their book bags in her office with the result that there is traffic in and out of the office all day long. She says, "The students truck in every morning. It looks like JFK or something."

HOW DO PRINCIPALS HANDLE THEIR WORKLOAD?

The effective principal works a sixty-hour week and more. The appearance of the principal at after-school and weekend events is needed for many reasons—it signifies this work of the staff and students is important, it improves control (people behave better when the principal is around), it ties the event to the work of the school, it ties the school to the community. But this makes for a long day.

Teachers recognize that principals work hard. They make statements like "my principal has worked so long and hard for all of us," "she gives 150 percent," and "her dedication is evident as long hours before and after her required duty are served." But probably few realize just how long the principal's work day is. One teacher commented, "Most teachers don't have a clue what the principal's day is like. I had the opportunity to be the assistant principal for the last three months; I knew my principal worked hard but I found out how hard." But maybe they do know. It seems that fewer and fewer teachers are preparing to become principals.

With such long days and work weeks it is a challenge for the principal to keep a balance between professional and personal life and to get needed time away from the job. There is no real support system for the principal in the school. She is on her own. It's very stressful to be constantly on front and center stage. The principal has to learn to do some things for herself once in a while. Without that there is the real threat of burnout on the job.

It's essential to have some time during the week that the principal sets aside for other activities, even if it is just to relax. Different strategies are adopted to accomplish this. Some use exercise programs as a stress reliever. Some set aside time to relax and laugh, perhaps finding a partner to help in this. Some connect with other principals with whom to share thoughts.

It takes a very supportive and understanding family. One principal in the study told the story about his son who always resented the fact that as he was growing up everywhere they went people would come up to them on school business. One day the son came home and said he finally got some payoff from having his dad as principal. He went to buy a used car, agreed on a price with the salesman, and then had the dealer knock $600 off the price. It turned out that the dealer appreciated all his dad had done for him as his high school principal.

Often the family must feel like the principal member of the family needs a name tag for those times at home. Many family meals are missed. Family members often go along to school events but even then they don't see much of the principal mom, dad, or spouse because she needs to touch base with all the different groups who are at the event. This may involve sitting in different places during each period of an athletic contest or moving about to speak to all those performing at an event. And, of course, family members are not spared the criticism that will inevitably be directed at the principal and are in fact often the target of it. This can be especially hard for young children at school. It takes a family that shares the principal's passion for the job and commitment to the education of all the children in the school.

Why do principals stick with a job where they have to work so hard? They love it. They feel a deep sense of mission that through their work they can touch many lives in a positive way. They can help students and their families as well as members of their staffs to find more success in life. They can help them through hard times and crises. For those who seek a daily challenge the principal's job is a perfect fit. It's an exciting and rewarding job making a difference for kids.

What does all this tell us about the strengths of those who are effective principals? Obviously they enjoy the opportunity of holding a job that basically is a "24 x 7" position. They want to be at the center of things. They are people of high energy and high stamina. They gain energy from almost constant interaction with others. Investing in others is rewarding for them. They gain energy by working to solve problems. They want to wrap themselves totally in their job. They like making things work. They enjoy being active and involved. They have a secure self-image which enables them to deal with the frequent challenges they face. When you talk with them they tell you how fortunate they are to be principals. First and foremost they want to be in a position to influence many people in a positive way. And they are.

"None of the days are the same so it never gets stale nor does it get routine nor ever gets so you know what the next day is going to be like. So I guess you have to like change to be a principal. I love problem solving and I love connecting and I love building relationships and love expanding and seeing other ways to make a difference. It feeds my soul. It isn't only an intellectual and emotional experience. It's a soul experience, because you know you make a difference. You can see this connection. You can see other people learning. Getting community people in on it, you see their joy and they like making a difference too. It's interesting how you can see the partnerships that are going to flourish right away and you also begin to realize which ones aren't going to go anywhere and so you just let go, you just let them die a natural death. But when you see that there's a potential to move into something else you nurture those and they grow beyond your wildest beliefs. That's what's really fun because you can't predict where it will go and you get to watch it grow on its own and have a life of its own really. It's part of being part of a learning organization that is changing, evolving. And I like change but I don't have to change jobs to experience that because this job changes all the time anyway."

3

WHAT'S THE EFFECTIVE PRINCIPAL LIKE?

What's an effective principal like as a person? Are there characteristics that describe effective principals that can help us to spot them? Or is this a very individualistic thing? While it certainly is the case that such principals have strong individual qualities, we found that they also have much in common.

OPTIMISM IS PRESENT IN LARGE DOSES

They know they can do the job. They know they can make a difference. To be an effective principal one has to believe that she can accomplish things. "If we as principals don't believe it can happen, it won't, and that's deadly for the school." If the principal doesn't believe that she can help things to turn out well then she is not a principal who applies positive psychology to her work.

You hear it said that we should see problems as opportunities. Effective principals really do. Problems provide the avenue to make things better. They provide ways to help bring out the best in people. Effective principals believe there is an answer to every problem and that they will come up with it. Their mind-set is that there is always a better way to do things. As one put it, "You have to make up in your mind early before you start the day that every problem you face has a solution, a reachable solution."

Effective principals can be identified by their optimistic approach to their work. Optimism is present even in the most dire situations.

It's important for the principal to be a visible optimist. The effective principal communicates to students, staff, and parents that she believes in the best in them and expects the best of them. "I think people look to us to be optimistic. Because if we are not, how can we expect those with whom we work to be?"

COMPETITIVE JUICES RUN STRONG

Effective principals are competitive. When asked where they are on a scale of competitiveness from one (low) to five (high), most immediately respond "five." As one said, "I'm only competitive during waking hours." Another stated, "If we could compete in 'Tiddlywinks' we'd do it."

They view competition as an opportunity for people to become their best, not as win–lose competition. They want their schools to get better and better. They want their schools to be the best in their district, the state, the nation. They want all other schools to be good, also, but for theirs to be the best. If someone tells them they can't accomplish something, that motivates them even more. They want to win the game—and the game is to have a school where students and staff are highly successful and where this is recognized by the community. Being competitive to the principal means you must always strive for improvement.

"I think the competition is against the bar. You are continually raising the bar. I had to jump the bar so I could raise it. I want the teacher to continually raise the bar for the kids."

Some of the principals in this study work in high-stakes testing states. Most, perhaps all, believe that high-stakes testing is unsound educationally. They see this approach as narrowing the curriculum to outcomes that are easily measured and making it more difficult for teachers to work with and value students as individuals. They are concerned that high-stakes testing will create a permanent underclass of young people who will not complete high school. But they have figured out how to make the high-stakes testing in which their schools are involved into a good thing. That's a reflection both of their optimism and their competitiveness. They have done this by making the raising of test scores a school project. Let's compete with ourselves to be better! They have made it a community effort and have focused on positive steps toward improvement. Teachers have joined together to develop routes to good test scores. Teachers and students have worked together to carry out these plans. Progress of all kinds has been celebrated (see chapter 6 for much more on celebrating).

When high-stakes testing came to one elementary school in a community of 250,000 people, the school did not do well compared with other schools in the district. This was a school where more than 90 percent of the students qualify for free or reduced lunch, where many students attend for whom English is not their first language or really even their language at all—characteristics all too often associated with low test scores. As one teacher at the school put it, "For families in a survival mode, reading and writing practice are not priorities." Under the leadership of an exceptionally dedicated principal the school made the commitment to narrow the test-score gap and to tolerate no excuses for not doing so. The challenge gave the staff energy as they worked to discover the support each student needed to improve. Taking advantage of some available grant money and resources at the local university, a plan was designed to make a difference. Curriculum changes were made, intense one-on-one instruction provided, and frequent testing carried out to monitor progress and to direct instructional efforts. Summer programs were added to provide extra help.

The results were dramatic. Discipline referrals dropped significantly as students began to feel more successful. Families were involved more effectively in the work of the school. Within a year, reading and math achievement improved significantly. High-stakes testing was harnessed to bring about school improvement.

"You can make it very unifying. When we were labeled as a low performing school it was very shocking but it became a real motivator for us. It made us link up with people we hadn't linked up with before. Helps you seek new areas of support. What I've noticed is that it gives schools like ours from very low income areas and our students a kind of parent. The government becomes their parent, demanding things for the kids that they didn't have access to before. We made it into a support for our children. But in raising our test scores we will never lose sight of the importance of socio-emotional development of our students for that is critical. Our teachers will find a way to focus on that regardless. You just have to believe they will."

Will there ever be a time when effective principals believe their schools have arrived? No. In this sense they are perfectionists, always striving to promote educational experiences for their students. They are always competing with today's level of performance to make it better.

REFLECTING IS A HABIT

Effective principals are reflective. Despite their hectic schedules these principals find time to reflect on what they are doing. That's their work orientation. They do this in different ways. Some set aside specific times to review their day and their week and to think about the day ahead. Some do it exercising or driving to and from work. One principal indicated that she had intentionally taken a job in a school some distance from her home so she would have ample drive time for reflection. Their reflection involves both review of what has happened and rehearsal for what may happen.

Reflection is necessary to allow fresh new ideas to develop. These take time to evolve but spring out of the principal's daily experiences. Principals need to be very broadly based because they deal with so many kinds of issues and situations. Their job is experience-intensive, but experience can only be instructive if you have time to think about it. Some find that what they call "thinking out loud" helps them to sort through things. If you don't learn from experience every day, you are soon behind.

Effective principals want teachers to be reflective, too. To support this and to help them frame issues for consideration require patience and tolerance. Many issues do not resolve themselves quickly and the principal needs to be able to live with the ambiguity the reflective process produces. If a principal can't do that, she will probably be an unhappy principal.

CHEERLEADING IS A STRONG TRAIT

Effective principals are cheerleaders. This was the single most stated descriptor the principals in this study applied to themselves. The principal sets the tone for the school and does this by attending to positive actions and behaviors and encouraging, encouraging, encouraging. It is not just a matter of being positive, but also of being less negative. Gallup's study of eight hundred outstanding leaders in both private and public organizations revealed that they make fewer negative comments than less successful leaders. In fact their ratio of positive to negative words is as great as four to one. This would seem to describe effective principals as well.

If the principal is not cheering, it is doubtful others will be. Cheerleading both reflects the principal's attitude and creates a positive attitude as well. The principal can make or break the school through the attitude she brings to her work. Effective principals do not let negative thinking and people drag them down. It is a challenge to always be up, but it's a challenge these principals meet.

Part of being a cheerleader is bringing a sense of humor to work. Sharing a laugh helps every situation. Finding humor in difficult situations often makes them more manageable.

Effective principals specialize in creating hope and aspirations. They are in the job of building pride. They let people know what is expected of them but do so in an encouraging manner—"I know you can do this!" The ability to motivate staff, students, and parents is a primary tool of the effective principal. This kind of principal pulls people up.

The effective principal is not in the job to seek recognition for herself. She has to understand herself, be comfortable with herself, and know what kind of person she is. She must not take herself too seriously. She has to be secure enough with herself to take the "slings and arrows" that inevitably come with the job. If the principal's focus is on her own ego and status, she probably is not a very good principal. Her focus must always be on providing recognition to others. To provide recognition to others requires the principal to be a good listener. She must be able to sit back and let others succeed. She has to know when to intervene and when to let the situation ride. She does not let situations become personal. This attitude is best stated by one of the study's principals: "Everybody who goes into the principalship has to have some degree of ego. But I think you have to check that ego at the door. I'm here to make other people the star."

The effective principal establishes an environment that brings out the best in all. In rating her principal, one teacher stated, "I know this seems a little too positive, but you'd have to come here to see what a truly great place this is." This describes how teachers feel about working in a school led by an effective principal.

The effective principal loves being a principal. She believes it is certainly one of the best jobs there is. It's something about which she is passionate. She loves the opportunity to help kids succeed. She enjoys the opportunity to speak for the school.

WHAT ARE THEY LIKE?

These then are critical strengths of effective principals who practice positive psychology. They are optimistic in the way they approach their work. This enables them to deal with the many situations they encounter in a positive way. They convey this optimism to all in the school in a way that leads others to be optimistic as well. They are competitive. They want nothing to stand in the way of student learning. They want their schools to be the best. They want to defeat anything that stands in the way of that outcome. They are reflective. Even though they are frequently called upon to act on the spur of the moment, they develop strategies that enable them to review and think carefully about what they are doing. They are cheerleaders and remain positive in even the toughest situations. This helps set an upbeat tone for the school. This tone establishes the belief that things can be done. And perhaps most important of all, these principals love their jobs and appreciate the opportunity to serve in such a leadership role.

4

WHAT GUIDES THE WORK OF THE PRINCIPAL?

What guides the work of the effective principal? Vision. Effective principals are very clear about the mission of their schools. In this they are consistent with a basic tenet of positive psychology that basing your work on a concept of the "good life" leads to success. The mission that the effective principal sees for her school is her concept of the good life for that school.

Schools exist for students. This may seem like the proverbial "no brainer," but it is not the belief that drives decisions in all schools. To the effective principal, all decisions and actions must be made with the welfare of students in mind. Being totally clear about the school's mission enables all resources to be focused on promoting it. Through their actions and communications effective principals keep their vision before all in the school all of the time. Keeping the school focused on the vision is an important asset of the effective principal.

One of the biggest challenges in running a successful school is maintaining focus. Students expect structure, as do teachers. The proper supporting structure enables them to do their best work. The school's vision helps provide that structure—a focus on acceptance and achievement. Here's how that works: "If you develop a common mission with a shared philosophy you will always be able to return to it when you are facing that diversity and those issues that tend to surface, whether they are curriculum issues, budgetary issues, or social issues. You will be able to regroup and reflect on the mission and the common ground."

There must be a clear vision for the school. Effective principals believe this strongly. The principal must be aware of her own beliefs and have a course to follow to realize them. This is what provides direction for her work. This is how she is able to respond consistently to the hundreds of situations she encounters, using them to move forward toward her goals. Looking at the principal logs in chapter 2, it is clear that if the principal does not have a clear direction for her work she will easily become consumed by the many "fires" that have to be fought. Principals with a clear vision for their schools use each situation to express that vision.

KEEPING THE VISION VISIBLE

Effective principals talk about their vision for the school all the time. They believe that it is important that staff, students, and the community know what they stand for. No day goes by without the principal bringing the vision to people's attention several times. It would not be uncommon for this to happen a dozen or more times during a day. Contrary to what happens in many organizations where the mission statement collects dust on some shelf, the mission in the effective principal's school is visible at all times.

The principal frames her comments about situations in terms of the vision. She puts notes in the school's daily bulletin. She has a "vision phrase," which is frequently repeated. She sends quotes and references to support the vision to teachers via e-mail. She includes vision statements in newsletters to parents. She puts up signs and posters around the building that include vision phrases. She focuses staff meetings on the vision. Students listen to a speaker who talks about the vision.

One school prints its mission statement and goals on a business card, which each student and parent is given at the beginning of each school year. Students and staff are encouraged to memorize the mission statement and goals. Large posters with the same information are posted in all classrooms, offices, and hallways.

What Does a Mission Statement Look Like?

How is the vision for the school stated? While the content of mission statements tends to be similar from school to school, how the vision is stated

Fontenelle Excels

In a community of learners
where STUDENTS DISCOVER
and
ADULTS REDISCOVER
THE JOYS OF LEARNING

GOAL I: I will read and write well.

GOAL 2:   I will learn math skills and be able to solve math problems.

GOAL 3:   I will use science to discover, make guesses and see if they
               are right.

GOAL 4:   I will learn to use the computer.

GOAL 5:   I will learn to be a friend, make good choices and be a good
               citizen in our world.

_____

Student Signature

Figure 4.1.   Fontenelle Mission Statement.

varies considerably. Here are some examples of the diversity of ways that the vision is expressed.

Mission of Lincoln High School

Lincoln High School is committed to preparing each student to use multiple perspectives and individual talents to live, learn, and work in a diverse society.

Our Vision of LHS

As a multicultural learning community we will provide for our students and staff a safe, fair, and inclusive learning environment where:

Each student is given an equal opportunity to grow in knowledge, skills, and responsible behaviors, to make positive life choices, and to become a life-long learner with the academic skills to continue education after high school.

Each student is given an equal opportunity to develop skills in leadership, thinking, and communication as well as the social and personal skills needed to work with others to solve life problems.

Each student will become a productive citizen in a culturally diverse, global community.

The Brentano Academy Pledge

(said each morning by the students after the pledge to the flag)

I pledge to be responsible for my own actions, words, and deeds.

I will use "manner words" such as please, thank you, and excuse me.

I will listen when others speak and will not interrupt the person who is speaking.

I will give only appropriate, positive comments.

I will always be willing to lend a helping hand.

I will respect the property of others.

I will speak in a voice appropriate to the situation.

I will always be ready and willing to learn.

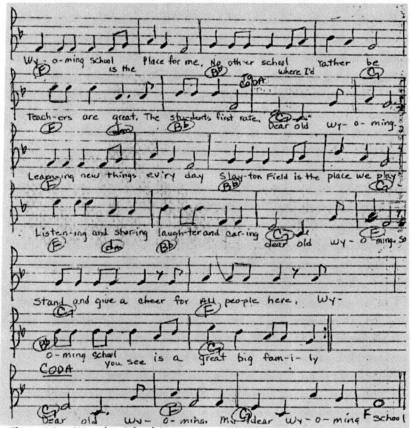

Figure 4.2. Wyoming School Song.

Wyoming School Song

By Jennie Maneri and Carmela Valles

(Can you visualize the students, as young as kindergarten age, joining hands and singing this school vision statement?)

IT'S THE STUDENTS

Regardless of how the vision is stated, it must focus on students. Through the vision the staff conveys to students that nothing comes before them.

"Kids first" might well be the watchword of effective principals. The school has to be a place where kids feel valued. For some it is a refuge from the rest of their lives where they do not feel valued. School is the one institution through which almost every child passes. The school must therefore have an uncompromising commitment to each child. One principal stated it this way: "Parents are sending you the only kids they have. They aren't keeping their best kids at home. So these are the kids with whom we must succeed. The parents are counting on us. The kids are counting on us."

The vision must reflect the notion that every student can succeed. This is a nonnegotiable position with effective principals. Implementation of the vision includes letting students know that the staff wants them to go home each day feeling successful and a little bit smarter than when they came to school that day.

The atmosphere in the school must be one in which all—students, staff, and community—can feel that they can achieve and are valued. That is much more likely to happen when all in the school subscribe to a clear vision of what they want the school to be.

The vision/mission statement is focused on the student. All students. What the environment will be like for students; what students will learn, both academically and socially; the ideal of creating a learning community; how successful schools want to be viewed by their constituents.

The school's vision is not always written down. In some schools it is more talked about and felt rather than printed. For example, at one elementary school the daily goal is reducing the achievement gap for poor and minority students by meeting each child's unique learning needs. All understand and can express this goal but it is not written down. This goal has mobilized the staff and given them the energy necessary for success. The key thing is that the vision/mission drives what people in the school do. Their work is integrated around it.

BUILDING THE VISION

Building the vision is a key activity. What is wanted is a collective vision that evolves from year to year as the group becomes more and more vision centered. The discussion involved in building the vision may be as important as the vision statement itself as it is through the discussion that the internalizing of the vision takes place. The vision needs to set expectations that all work toward. Vision building is also community building and culture building. It pulls the staff together. There may well be disagreements in the process of vision building. But these can be handled positively and, in fact, can help to clarify the vision.

Vision building starts with the principal's beliefs; it has to start with something to talk about. These beliefs, however, must be stated as a starting point. The process followed should expand on and sharpen those beliefs as they become the vision of the school community. The principal has to keep the process moving through providing notes of the discussions, framing agendas, talking with people individually to keep their attention on the task, delegating assignments to keep people involved, and scheduling meetings. Some will not want to work on vision building, perhaps from their previous experiences of such discussions leading nowhere. The principal's enthusiasm will be necessary to encourage involvement.

In the process of building the vision the statement being developed may get complicated as many ideas come forward. In the end, however, it becomes simple as the common element in these ideas—the centrality of the student—becomes clear. Written or not, the vision needs to be understood and internalized by the staff and even the students so that it guides their work.

Effective principals structure vision-building in a variety of ways. Some use faculty meetings for team-building. Some believe the first of the year is the time especially to focus on the vision as teachers and staff are especially optimistic and receptive then. Lots of carefully planned discussion is needed if the vision is to become meaningful to all. What are the most important outcomes we are seeking in our school? What do we want our school to be like? How will we describe success for our school? What are our strongest beliefs about our work as educators?

Effective principals are often assigned to schools that are not doing well. The starting point to improvement is always the establishment of a clear vision, and that's the first thing the principal works on. One principal faced with the task of turning around a low-performing school did this: "I pulled teachers, secretaries, aides, and janitors together for a daylong retreat. We talked about roadblocks for the school and how to get around them. We developed a motto that is now the school's rallying cry: 'Our School Is the Place to Be.' We say it constantly. We are clearly focused on student learning, that our school be a safe place for children, and we are committed to the partnership between home and school."

In fairly quick order this school realized increased achievement scores, decreased disciplinary problems, and increased parental involvement. The atmosphere improved once staff began to work together with a common plan and vision. Everyone got on the same page. They came together with a centralized focus and vision for how good the school could be. They had a belief that drove their work.

The way that effective principals work in this arena is remarkably similar to how C.E.O.s who are successful in turning around failing companies work. Gallup research has identified that these business leaders do visioning, focus on goals that are measurable, mentor people in terms of the vision, help people make sense of their experiences (i.e., why did this happen?), share their values constantly, and work to build a constituency.

How Do Teachers Perceive the Work of Principals in Establishing a Student-Oriented Vision?

"Dave's number one concern is doing what's best for kids." "Our school has been under a lot of pressure this year. Our principal has done a great job to mediate between all these groups and still keep children and what is best for them as the focus." "She is a positive leader with a great desire to touch the lives of children." "Her main focus is on kids receiving the best education possible." "My principal has high standards for both teachers and students and she never strays from this goal of excellence for all." "My principal has worked for ten years to develop a climate in our building of student achievement and student belonging." Clearly effective principals are strong advocates for a student-oriented vision for their schools.

Effective principals have strong beliefs about what schools can and must accomplish for students. They believe that the school must be committed to each student, regardless of what that student brings to school and how he or she performs. Every student can learn. It is the job of the school to find the path to help the student realize his or her learning potential. The emphasis is also on the student as a person. Effective principals want students to have academic success, but they also want them to become "better" people. Their view of what this includes is a student who has a positive self-image, who wants to continue to learn, and who treats others with respect. Effective principals believe you cannot separate the learner from the whole person. You have to be interested in both. You have to develop both.

An important strength of effective principals is their ability to be visionary about what their schools can be. This vision focuses on helping students succeed as learners. These principals are able to involve staff and students in this vision in a way that both incorporates their thinking and provides direction for action. Turning the vision into reality is the hallmark of success for the principal.

5

WHAT'S MOST IMPORTANT TO EFFECTIVE PRINCIPALS?

By now, the answer to the question "What's most important to the effective principal?" should be obvious. The effective principal has an unwavering commitment to the growth of the people in her school.

"I get up every morning and see the kids in my mind." "I am going to give all the kids my best shot because I want them to give me theirs." "I believe all children can learn. It's my job to establish the environment where that can happen." One teacher in reflecting on this commitment of her principal said, "Our principal has changed our school for the better into a school that puts children first."

HOW DO THEY HELP STUDENTS SUCCEED?

Their commitment to students is expressed in a number of ways. One is in never giving up on a student. The effective principal tries to find what it is that will help students succeed when they are struggling; what it is that is lacking in their lives in and out of school that may serve as an obstacle to school success. Sometimes this is frustrating because there appears no way to help the student, but the principal continues to try. Sometimes giving students one more chance "comes back and bites you on the back side" but that does not discourage the principal from continuing to try. When asked to talk about their successes, effective principals most often talk about the at-risk students who made it or the students with serious problems who turned around and licked those problems.

Part of helping students to succeed is making certain they come to school with a fair shot at success. This may include finding adequate clothing for them. That's something probably most principals have done. It may be to find a way for them to get needed dental care or inoculations. It may involve locating a place for them to live—there are school-age children without a place to live. It may involve working with students' families to help them provide better support to their children. It may involve hiring students to do little jobs such as cleaning up after a school event so they can earn much needed money for food or clothing. It may mean working to establish a breakfast program for the school because so many students are not able to have breakfast at home and thus do not come to school ready to learn. It may mean providing a Christmas gift for that child who will otherwise get none. Or a free yearbook for the student who cannot afford one. Maybe it's working with teachers or community groups to ensure that food baskets are provided for families who would otherwise go hungry. It may mean giving a student who has created problems an in-school suspension instead of suspension from school when he has no real home to go to. The effective principal sees all this as part of her job. It's part of her commitment to students.

Building relationships with students is a key element in the effective principal's commitment. Connecting at a personal level with students enables the principal to go back and help the student grow in many ways. "If you're willing to open up a little bit of yourself to students this will foster a strong relationship." Students must be helped as individuals. As one principal stated, "I suspect that if you kept only a single standard for all kids and you never made an individual exception, you would not succeed with many kids." Effective principals go out of their way to find opportunities to visit with students and to know about them individually.

The number one concern of the effective principal is the students. This is what drives them in their work. It is the desire and the opportunity to touch children's lives that makes the job fulfilling for the effective principal. Their real work is with the students, even though there is much "other" work required in their jobs.

HOW DO THEY HELP STAFF TO SUCCEED?

The effective principal also has a strong commitment to the teachers and other staff of her school. Effective principals believe that the single most important thing they do is to hire the right people. Principals need to be really, really good at hiring.

What do effective principals look for in a teacher? Someone who is open, honest, hard working, and energetic, and who does not have a lot of emotional baggage. Someone who shares the principal's commitment to students and who is determined students will learn. Someone who has a passion to help students grow. Someone who can help carry out the school's vision. People who like students—you can't teach that; it has to be there in the beginning. Teachers who are enthusiastic about everything. Teachers who are smart. Teachers who are courageous. Teachers who work well with colleagues. Teachers who want to continue to learn and who can accept change. Teachers who have empathy. Teachers with compassion and common sense. Teachers who believe they are bringing something to the school that will make it a better school. Teaching done right is a brutally hard job. It takes great people to do it right.

"They have to have fire in their bellies. I hired six new ones this year that I think are just going to be excellent. I saw it in their eyes. I saw it in their tone of voice and their mannerisms. They want to be around kids. They want to have an impact on kids. They want to teach."

Once you have these teachers on board you need to help them build capacity and empower them. In some ways teachers and other staff are the principal's students. She must build a strong relationship with them and continue to provide support and training for them on an ongoing basis. Once you have delegated you cannot just step aside. You must continue to provide guidance and support. It's the principal's job to make certain that teachers are successful in the classroom.

How do effective principals work with teachers to help them improve? "Before they can hear anything you say, you have to prove that you understand their situation and what they're doing and how they make decisions. And so the first part is just being beside them, learning what it is that they're doing and understanding their frustrations, their loves, their passion. You know you have accomplished that when they start sharing things that are hard—what they are afraid of—and then you can become a partner with them. You can't go in with a template of what a good teacher looks like and then measure them against the template. Teachers are each unique and you have to understand where they are coming from and what is scary to them and also what their dreams are before you can make a difference.

"So building that trust, building that deep understanding, allows you to tell them something about their teaching that they didn't know themselves so they know that you are adding to them. That's how I know if I've really made a difference. If I go and observe and we have a conversation and then when I write up what that conversation was about and then I get a response from them like, 'I didn't even know I did this, you've taught me something I didn't know about myself before' then I've gotten that gold nugget. Then I know they'll be able to listen to other things from me because I've taught them something about themselves that they didn't know before and then you know you can move on. And they realize that you are really tuning in on who they are and what they do and everything about them. And it takes awhile. Principals need to be direct and genuine and transparent and so if you see something that could make a difference quickly, you just have to say that out loud and not worry about how it falls but watch carefully after you say it how it impacts the person. People will say I can't believe how you talk to the teachers, you're so direct aren't you worried about hurting their feelings or something? And I say, I guess it's just how we have a relationship and so I don't have to worry about that.

"I worked with a teacher who didn't know for certain whether he was still growing as a teacher after seven years on the job. 'Is this the profession for me?' he was asking. We started by using our regular evaluation process to work through this. Did some portfolio-building and journaling. He decided to shadow some other more experienced teachers and to do some reading about teaching as a career. He set some new goals that spurred him on. We worked through all this together. It takes trust on both sides. You have to be honest and you have to maintain the confidentiality of the discussions."

Thus a trusting partnership is essential to helping others grow. It has to be a patient process with the principal providing support and direction throughout. The process must be focused on what is best for the teacher with the principal as helper.

All those who work at the school are important: Teachers, secretaries, custodians, aides, bus drivers, and more. Each plays an important role in the environment of the school. All need to be responding to students consistently. All are part of the package that makes up a good school. One principal talked about having the "most friendly sweeper in the world" and how important that was for her school. This person's consistent smile and good cheer brings out the same in those she encounters. She has an influence on the school that goes far beyond what might be considered to be her job description. The right staff people can make valuable contributions to the success of the school. They often will relate to students in ways that teachers cannot, coming at them from a different perspective.

It is important that teachers and other staff believe they have a voice in what's going on in the school. The principal should view herself as the lead teacher, not an authority figure. It's the principal's job to provide teachers the support and resources they need to get their jobs done. The principal not only must listen to teachers but also must encourage them to share ideas. Whenever possible she should act on the suggestions that come from staff. Teachers and staff should be encouraged to take responsibility. The principal must endeavor to establish a supportive environment for them. When the teachers are secure in their place in the school they then can give their most to help students learn. This also produces a situation in which teachers can continue to learn and take risks on behalf of students. Effective principals encourage staff development and push very hard for teachers to have the time to talk through and then implement what they are learning.

The effective principal works to produce a school environment that will lead excellent teachers to want to work in that school. Most of the principal's job is dealing with relationships. The principal works to set an attitude and to empower people. She is positive and supportive and emphasizes the capabilities of others. She works to keep people "pumped up" and to smooth over differences and difficulties. Her trust in each staff member allows each to provide quality instruction. Human relations are a huge, huge part of the principal's work. Effective principals look for ways for people to become winners. They encourage staff members to do their best every day. If the staff is engaged in their work, so too will be the students.

Effective principals help teachers and staff see the big picture. This is something that teachers and staff often struggle with because they are so involved in their individual parts of the school. But if they are going to be effective in helping all students to succeed they must understand this big picture.

Similarly, the principal helps teachers understand changes and how to incorporate them in their work in a positive manner. The current emphasis on assessment is a good example of this dynamic. Teachers are often not certain the new assessment emphasis is necessary and fear that it may hinder what they are doing. The task of the principal is to help them learn to use assessment to improve what they are doing.

ENERGY FOR THE PRINCIPAL

Effective principals draw energy from supporting students and staff. This is what keeps them going. They make comments like, "I feel wealthy because I know all these people and have a connection with them" and "I have been blessed with the opportunity to work with these students and teachers."

The emphasis these principals place on supporting students and staff and building community is consistent with what research on business outcomes has demonstrated. Companies where employees report positive workplace satisfaction, opportunities for personal development, and friendships at work are those that achieve higher levels of customer satisfaction and employee retention as well as productivity and profitability. Results are better when the work environment is positive.

Effective principals are committed to all those in their schools. They believe in them. They see their role as providing the support and resources to help students and staff succeed. They get great joy in so doing.

6

WHAT DO EFFECTIVE PRINCIPALS CELEBRATE?

When effective principals are asked what they celebrate, the answer is likely to be something like "everything." All the behaviors they want to grow are celebrated.

These principals love to celebrate. They celebrate progress toward the vision they have for their schools. They celebrate happenings important to their students, staff, community, and nation. They celebrate what they want to encourage.

They understand that celebration both identifies what the desirable behaviors and actions are for those in the school and reinforces these behaviors and actions when they occur. They understand that when students and staff feel good about how they are doing and how their school community is doing they move toward doing better. They create positive behavior by paying attention to positive behavior. This is a direct application of the "broaden-and-build model" that has been found to be so successful in improving performance in many kinds of organizations.[1] This model explains that positive emotions that are experienced by people at work build their personal resources and behavioral repertoires to perform in an increasingly positive manner in a broader set of circumstances. Thus doing well and having that recognized are prerequisites to doing better.

Academic accomplishment is celebrated, but in a broader sense than commonly considered. For example, several schools in this study give special recognition to students who do not make the honor roll but who work hard during the semester or show improvement. Success in and contributions to musical, speech, athletic, and all other cocurricular activities of the school are noted. Good attendance figures (for both students and teachers) are celebrated. Doing things for the common good, helping others out, giving one's best effort in whatever one undertakes in the school—all of these are given attention. Some principals make a deliberate effort to honor every student in the school for something she or he has done during each semester.

Effective principals focus on growth. They believe all students will grow if the environment is supportive. These principals see and recognize growth where others may only see that the student is still behind. They build the environment that is best for growth.

Celebration is a chief teaching method for the effective principal.

HOW DO THEY CELEBRATE?

Parents coming to the school to visit is a cause for celebration. This points out how important parent support is to student success. In one school, parents graduating from English as a Second Language classes provides another reason for celebrating; this tells these parents who did not experience schooling as children in this country that the school values them. Other parent accomplishments are noted as well. Through this the school indicates its investment in parents as well as in their children. Community accomplishments are noted to point out to all the close ties between school and community.

Getting off to a good start in the school year or bringing the semester to a strong close are times for celebrating. Effective principals look for causes for celebration.

Faculty meetings become a celebration of the work that teachers do. Teachers' accomplishments are recognized. Teachers are asked to tell about or demonstrate something they have done. Their teaching is recognized and celebrated. Meetings are started with the question "Is there somebody you would like to praise or thank for something they have done?" One principal holds what she calls an "Evening of Excellence," in which each teacher is asked to share something that she or he does regularly in class. Recognizing teachers in ways such as these helps them learn to know and appreciate each other. These kinds of celebrations provide a positive focus for teaching.

Effective principals find ways to celebrate on a periodic basis. "Every Friday around lunch we have a huge assembly and give out 12, 15, 20 awards." "We celebrate each week that goes by every Friday morning." "We have performances that come down from the middle school to the elementary school—like a Renaissance rally but we do it every Friday. Our attendance is always highest on that day."

Lots of avenues are found to recognize good performance.

"We put pictures up on the board monthly—eight big pictures; one from each class."

"Classes that have perfect attendance for the week can have a party at the end of the week."

"We have a student day in the spring where we just celebrate students. We contract with a carnival company."

"I take photos and blow them up to poster size and plaster them around the school."

"We put stickers on report cards to point out good performance."

"We have flagpole assemblies where we bring everybody outside and have the school band or chorus perform and have presentations made."

"I walk around with a camera all the time in school and take pictures of good things happening and then make collages every month of these pictures."

"We have dignitaries to our school to help us celebrate what we do."

"We have great success with academic pep rallies."

"We have an hour-of-excellence dinner where we reward students who have perfect attendance, students with no discipline notices, and students who make the honor roll."

"If the speech team does really well at the speech meet then we'll probably have an evening where we invite the community to come in and listen to these kids. A pie-and-coffee kind of thing."

"We have a limousine lunch program. We set up a 'caught doing good' program and if we see students picking up trash, doing extra homework, doing something nice for a teacher or a fellow student, something like that we will give them a little card to put in a drawing. We pull out ten names a month and those selected get to go in a limo to wherever they want to eat lunch. They always pick McDonalds or some place like that. We have received so much good press for that program. It's very productive and positive for the school and creates much good behavior."

"We web cast our prom and graduation so relatives in other states can share in these happy celebrations."

"The first day of school for all freshmen we have a pizza party on the front lawn to celebrate their joining our school community."

Food seems to be part of many celebrations. Somehow food creates a bond. This works for staff as well as students. Pizza parties are always a hit. One school whose colors are blue and white has blue lemonade in the cafeteria on celebration days. Another had blue lemonade to celebrate being named a "Blue Ribbon School."

Sometimes the principal becomes the fun "target" of a celebration. Perhaps it's a pie thrown in the principal's face when students meet a certain learning goal. "Last year we met our reading goal as a school. So I dyed my hair green, put on green nail polish, and a green and black polka dot dress for the celebration. The kids thought it was fun."

RECOGNIZING TEACHERS AND STAFF

Effective principals focus on recognizing staff as well as students.

"The teachers who have done something special—I will give them a certificate that says this is good for $50 worth of materials for your classes."

"Every other month we do an extended lunch to give us time to talk about what teachers are doing."

"We give out little trophies for most valuable teachers, rookie teachers, and other reasons that are chosen by the staff as a whole. Everyone enjoys these awards."

"I put 'Thousand Dollar' candy bars in teachers' boxes along with a note of thanks for something they have done."

"Little gifts, not expensive, just little trinkets and gifts go a long way."

"I give roses each month based on suggestions from the staff. Roses are for those who have gone out of their way to care about each other and their students. And radishes are for those of us who have done the goofiest things that we can laugh at. These make us all human."

"I have a weekly Monday Memo where I talk about the great things our teachers do."

"I started nominating my teachers for every award that comes across my desk."

"My initials are MM so I have personally always brought M&M's to school. I notice that after a long week my M&M dispenser goes down quickly. It's a way of letting everyone know I am thinking about them."

"In one school each graduating senior invites a favorite teacher she or he had in elementary, middle, or high school to attend commencement and walk in with them."

"There are times which are high stress times for teachers, like report card time. Those are the times when you do just little fun things for the staff to recognize their work."

"When we have a teacher who is retiring we set up a time where we really honor them. We talk about the legacy they are leaving us and I really challenge all of us to live up to that legacy."

"At the end of the year we are all tired and a little down. So one of the things I started doing was making a list of all of our achievements that we accomplish throughout the year and sharing it with the staff. When I would bring that to the forefront, the staff would say, 'No wonder we're tired, we have had a great year.' "

Special situations call for special recognition. One principal, whose teachers were on strike with the others in their district, brought doughnuts to the teachers on the picket line each morning. Another had a Kool-Aid party for the custodians who were painting bleachers on a 100-degree day. Another school thanked the custodians for their special work in getting the school ready for the year by holding a dinner for them and their spouses. Teachers dressed in tuxes and served as waiters and hosts.

PRIVATE CELEBRATIONS

Celebrations do not have to be public in nature. A principal in the study put it this way: "I try to go around and talk with individuals everyday and find something positive that they are doing to talk about. Sometimes I think these personal celebrations are more meaningful than the public ones." An activity such as visiting a class is a kind of recognition for both the teacher and students involved. Going down the hallway and saying "Good job" or "Congratulations" to those you see can be very important. A powerful way to recognize staff or students is through asking them to take on responsibility for an important activity or process. This conveys confidence in their work and abilities.

Note-writing is a frequent activity for effective principals. A memo or thank-you note to those who do good things for the school is generally greatly appreciated. Some principals set aside a certain period each day (perhaps 15 minutes) to write such notes. Another approach is this: "I buy one of those little novelty pads of paper that have 50 pieces and I know that every month I have to write 50 praise letters. If I'm not done on the last day of the month, I am at school until I finish."

IT WORKS

Most likely top principals' emphasis on celebration is an outgrowth of both their personalities and experience. Whether they realize it or not what they are doing is well supported by research. Studies have shown that even small positive interventions can produce important effects on workers in many fields. Employee engagement is a critical factor in organizational success, and such engagement is supported by the approach that effective principals take to their jobs.

Celebrating to recognize good performance is an important practice for the effective principal. Every school should have some kind of discretionary fund for the principal to use to support celebrations. Perhaps every principal should have a camera to record important events and activities as well. Through celebrations the principal recognizes the best in students and staff and helps them see it as well. Through celebrations the principal helps people move toward the school's vision and to continue to seek higher performance. Through celebrations, the effective principal holds before all in the school what the desired behaviors are.

NOTE

1. B. L. Frederickson, "The Role of Positive Emotions in Positive Psychology: The Broaden-and-Build Theory of Positive Emotions." *American Psychologist* 56 (2001): 218–26.

HOW DO EFFECTIVE PRINCIPALS DEAL WITH ADVERSITY?

Even though effective principals are optimistic people who strive always to display a positive frame of mind in their work they do, of course, encounter adversity—actually lots of adversity from a variety of sources. Looking at what causes adversity for them and how they deal with it reveals even more about why these principals are effective leaders.

The daily life of the principal can certainly create adversity. Not every decision works out. There is too much work to be done. People quarrel. People refuse to look for solutions to their unhappiness. The days are long. Crises happen, including events as serious as a grave illness or the death of a student or teacher. People the principal depends on or for whom she has given a second, or third, chance let her down. It's a job with lots of pressures and many things that can go wrong. In many ways principals catch grief from all sides and people pass their problems along to them. They are like lightning rods that are hit often. When something goes wrong, which inevitably will happen, the principal gets blamed. When people are unhappy—students, staff, or community members—they most often pass their unhappiness along to the principal.

A major source of discouragement for effective principals is not being able to help some students in their schools. It's extremely frustrating to them to see a student who is really hurting but to have no place to go to get him or her the help needed. Some students come to school seemingly with more than two strikes against them. Principals, as well as teachers and other staff members, do much to try to help these students have a fighting chance but sometimes what they can do is not enough. Standing by and watching young people fail at school and life is very depressing for the dedicated principal. It's tough also to deal with people, organizations, and institutions that seem to have lost faith in these young people who are struggling, or who perhaps have given up struggling, against great odds.

Effective principals may also be disheartened by what they perceive as lack of public support for schools. In many communities, they sense a general distrust of the educational system. Often it seems to principals that those in the community who are the least trusting have the least current firsthand knowledge of what the schools are actually like. A common reaction of effective principals is if we could just get members of the public into the schools to see what we are doing they would be impressed. The schools, perhaps like other institutions in our society, however, have often become targets of politicians, business leaders, religious leaders, and the media. Some states have adopted high-stakes testing programs, most over the objection of educators, which seem to these principals to be more punitive than educational. "We have had 122 months of the greatest expansion in the history of the world— economic expansion. Have you heard the school get congratulated for that? But in 1988 and 1989 when we had that recession what was the problem? The public schools weren't bringing enough people into the workplace." "About three or four days after we got back from getting a very prestigious national award for our school we found out our test-score average went down one point. And guess what? We heard about it in the press."

National polls such as the annual Gallup Poll for Phi Delta Kappa over and over reveal that citizens have confidence in the schools that serve their children but not in the schools of the nation as a whole. This is an interesting phenomenon, which in some ways just does not make sense. Perhaps this adds to the frustration that effective principals feel; that is, that some of the lack of public support they encounter is not even the result of anything their own schools have done or not done but rather something thought to be true about schools in general. The financial pressures that schools in many states have found themselves in coupled with the current anti-tax mood of the country ends up seeming to pit school against community in far too many situations. All these things are discouraging to the principal who is dedicated to the education of her students.

BOUNCING BACK

So how do effective principals deal with adversity and opposition? How do they bounce back from disappointment? For one thing these principals realize that people are watching to see how they handle adversity. Adversity, despite its negative nature, provides another teaching opportunity for the principal. It is especially important that those in the school see the principal handling disheartening situations in a positive way. It is especially important that the principal models keeping hope alive in all situations.

Effective principals come back from disappointment by focusing on their students. Especially, they look at those who need the help of the school to climb the mountains they are facing in their lives. Then the principal knows she can't get down but must continue to move forward. She gets to work.

One antidote for adversity is to visit classes. This is particularly a choice for elementary principals. Going to watch kindergarten students involved in learning is a guaranteed way to feel better about things ("If my staff can't find me they know to look in the kindergarten room."). It lights up the world with sunshine and happiness. Visiting classes gets you back to why you are in this business. Seeing the wonderful things that teachers and students do together is always a good pick-me-up. Often principals will get themselves involved in the classroom activities, especially with younger students.

Some use exercise as a way to deal with a tough day. Going to the gym and completing some physical activity provides a fresh start for many. Others find a way to take a short break. "I will tell my secretary, can you handle it for ten minutes? I then turn out the lights, turn on the light on my desk and get some little devotional book or something. I'll just take a break for a few moments." Hobbies help, but few principals have the time for them. One raises sheep on the side and "gives them an earful when things go wrong!" Obviously having a supportive family is an essential for the principal. Facing difficult situations is much easier when the principal has a healthy part of her life outside school on which to draw.

Often principals reflect on the successes experienced in their job when things get really tough. Some keep a good note file with messages of appreciation from students, former students, parents, and staff and read them again. "We can deal with this because we've taken enough pictures in our mind of successes that we have a back log. We don't take as many pictures of failures and we don't flip through that album."

The optimistic orientation of the effective principal helps too. She bounces back more easily because she is certain that things will get better. Things may look dark today but tomorrow will be better. "Mama says there will be days like this. You just chalk them up and get on with the next day." "I regroup and figure out how we can do it a different way. You have to punt sometimes and start over." Good humor is always an asset in dealing with the serious nature of many of the issues that are faced. When things do not go right it is an opportunity to learn how to make them better next time. Find something good about the situation and moving on rather than dwelling on it.

> "I love challenge. I love complexity. So I don't look at what happens at work as being stressful or hard. I look at it as something that really gives me energy rather than taking energy away. I love problem solving and being able to think out of the box. I love being able to say 'yes' as many times as I can. I try to always say yes and that there is a way to do it. I get to work. It's fun."

> "What keeps me going is focusing on the impact I can have on kids and teachers. It's the little things that make you feel good. Looking for progress. Going home thinking you have made one person's day a little better. Focus on the positive."

> "You have to find ways not to burn out from the stress. I try to do things to 'stir my soul.' Sometimes it's a big project like when our school built the Habitat for Humanity house. This was my way of focusing on something. Seeing a project through keeps you positive. But little things help too. Like going to a literature class and participating in book talks."

> "Long days are just natural. To get through them I try to set up little rewards for myself. Like taking a long walk around the building. Having something different for lunch. Listening to some favorite music. I try to get well organized for what I am going to do so I don't get a feeling of being frantic to get ready."

Things don't always go well for effective principals. This is the nature of the job. "I tell everybody who's considering going into administration, don't go into it if you're not planning on getting beat up because you will get beat up over and over." Part of it is the high expectations effective principals have for themselves and their schools. But they stay in character when encountering adversity. They remain optimistic. "Any time you have a setback, that's an opportunity to learn something." They remember their responsibility to model positive behavior for all in the school. And they continue to focus their attention on helping students.

8

WHAT MAKES THE EFFECTIVE PRINCIPAL FEEL SUCCESSFUL?

What gives effective principals a feeling of success in their work? What is it that makes the job worthwhile to them? Recognizing the high standards they bring to their work, what enables them to believe they are making progress? It should be no surprise that the answers to these questions revolve around the performance of students and staff.

There are things that happen every day that help principals know whether they are being successful. Do the students show that they are excited to be in school? Are the teachers enthusiastic, glad to be in the school? Do teachers choose to talk about ways to make students successful when they are together in venues such as teacher forums? Are the complaints to the principal significant to the lives of students and teachers?

There are many things that happen at school to give principals a feeling of joy. Some are brief positive events that happen throughout the day. "A sixth-grade boy came up and gave me a Valentine. Last year he spent more time in my office than I did. And it came to me, he was not spending time in the office any more." It's seeing the proverbial lightbulb go on for first- and second-grade students. You can just see these students smile when they learn something new, when they first get it. Or maybe it is when you see students taking on responsibility for themselves and for the school.

"The Kodak moments are the real important things that keep me going. You know, the sparkle in the eye for the kids or whatever it might be that the

kids accomplish. The same thing for teachers. When they make that professional stride."

"We were selected as America's best school one year by a national maga-
zine. That was incredibly wonderful. But probably the greatest successes are
little ones and when I look around I see. We had four or five students in special education programs who when they graduated ended up not only meeting our state standards but being in the ninetieth percentile as well as win-
ning national presidential academic fitness awards."

Being part of a school that makes a real difference for students is the ulti-
mate reward for top principals. As experts in their profession they believe
that they can quickly sense whether the school is a difference maker in students' lives.

"It's something you can sense when you walk into a building. You can
hear things happening. Inclusive and welcoming. Inviting. Laughter. That
the people in the building like the other people in the building. The kids and
the staff feel a niche. They belong. A lack of fear. There's a lot of love. Something that focuses on kids when you walk in. The kids like being in the building."

Working in such a school brings the satisfaction that you are doing what's
right for students. Teachers become better teachers. Students become better
students. And, ultimately, families become better families. Family self-esteem
increases as their child is successful at school.

Secondary principals find commencement to be a particularly moving
and exciting time. For many it is the single most rewarding moment in the
course of the year. It gives them a sense of pride to think that they played a
role in the success of these students. Male and female principals alike talk
about getting "teary eyed" at the graduation ceremonies. At this time students frequently show their appreciation for the support they have received.
Principals find this very meaningful.

Encountering students after they have graduated is also often a rewarding
experience for principals. Former students come up to them in places of
business, on the street, at athletic contests, and at other places or stop in to
see them in their offices at school. After they have been out of school for a
few years students often become more aware of how valuable their school experience was and how much support they received from their principal.
They also want to tell their principals about what they have accomplished in

life since school. This is particularly true for students who may have struggled some in school and want the principal to know that the faith she showed in them has paid off.

Effective principals always enjoy seeing their former students. It helps them realize the differences they have made in these individuals' lives. Attending class reunions is a favorite activity for many principals. When they hear from former students that something they did touched their lives in a positive manner, they know they are working in a noble profession.

These follow-ups do not always work out well. One principal reports, "One of my favorite kids that I had years ago is on death row. I wish I had known that he was changing and I could have tried something." Typically, he saw himself as wanting to continue to be of help.

Then there are the student projects and activities that bring cheer. In one school a student won a national academic award and selected the principal as the person to accompany him to Washington to receive his award. A student body voted for the king and queen for their junior/senior prom two noncommunicative, wheelchair-bound students. Opportunities like meeting with students and their teachers and parents backstage after the performance of a high school musical are appreciated, seeing the positive experience of six weeks of hard work for all of them providing real rewards.

In one school where three children had been struck by an intoxicated driver while coming to school in the morning, a "Students Against Drunk Drivers" group was started. Working on behalf of new drunken-driving legislation in their state, 1,600 kids marched to the legislature with one of the children who had been struck leading the march in his wheelchair. They put on a program for the governor and legislature. The legislation they supported was passed.

One high school developed a sister-school relationship with a high school in Japan. Student-sustained exchange programs have been conducted for the past ten years. It's truly a group project from which everyone learns.

Another school, which had performed poorly on the state testing program, decided to involve all its stakeholders in working to improve their standing. Students set goals and then worked to realize these goals. The focus was on all students, not just the upper echelon academically. Everyone worked together to prepare for the tests, and the following year the test results were much improved.

Success experiences come to principals in many ways. An article about a principal appeared in the local newspaper and many students brought copies of it to her. Then there are those letters received from former students that show up from time to time. One student sent his former principal an essay he had written at college about the person who had meant the most to him in life—and it was that principal. One principal received a standing ovation from his faculty for the way he handled a crisis situation. Another indicated that it made her feel great when her teachers enrolled their own children in the school even though they were from another attendance area.

A principal who had received a national honor relates the following story: "When it came out in the paper, one of the students that I'd had in one of my previous schools—who had had some difficulties, who was now working across the city—rode his bike from his place of work—he had no other form of transportation—to my school because he wanted to tell me he had seen it in the paper and he wanted to thank me for being a really good principal."

THERE ARE RICH REWARDS

Top principals talk about how rich the rewards are from doing their job:

"I think my health is better and my whole outlook on life is better when I am doing this. Trying to create things; there is something really heady about that."

"It's a challenge that pushes you physically, mentally, spiritually, and emotionally. I think we thrive on that. Each day is exciting. And so different. You never know what you are going to come across."

"There are so many rewards—whether it's dealing with teachers in each project or being the visionary that creates the project and finds the people that make it move. I find great rewards in dealing with kids and watching them grow over four years. Seeing what a neat, neat person a kid can become."

"It's almost frightening that when we are called upon to help plan funerals and do things that aren't normally thought of as something we would do. There is no other job where you are such an integral part of influencing a larger community because it goes so far beyond the school you are in."

"I've been a Legion baseball coach and have won the state tournament and various things. That's memorable. But you know I think seeing kids succeed—especially ones who didn't think they could—is the greatest. So is kids coming back to school to visit with you after they have graduated."

For some students the school is their best safe haven, their best chance for growth and success. "I think we see the greatest evidence of this over winter break when you leave for two weeks. Kids leave their routine, the daily lunch and breakfast program, the teachers and counselors who work with them in a group or individually. And they are gone and just come back after two weeks looking like they have lost a few pounds. They are a little disheveled, maybe a little dirtier or a little more tired. They are waiting at the school door for it to get unlocked at 6:30 in the morning on the first day back."

SUCCEEDING AGAINST THE ODDS

There are many forms of successes for effective principals. But for many the greatest victory is to see students succeed against heavy odds. This is best told in their words:

"A student we have invested four or five years of concentrated efforts in just finished his fifth grade this year. He weighs in excess of 270 pounds. His mother rejected him. He doesn't live at home all the time. He is labeled as oppositional defiant, has many acting-out behaviors. For a couple of years I felt almost like a bulldog rider because of his need to be physically restrained or removed because of endangering other students. And the success story is I came to the realization this year that he's turned the corner and he is resilient to the place that he will make it in spite of all those things. Everybody invested, not one person did it all, but the cumulative effect of handling with a kid made a world of difference when it would have been easier to have given up on him."

"Last year we had a student graduate who was a seven-year student in our high school. He ended up as a seven-year student because he got involved in drugs quite heavily. But he always kept coming back. And it was pretty exceptional to talk with his dad on graduation night and to see his entire family up there in the stands, and to listen to them cheer when he walked across the stage."

"One of the successes of my career was with a kid who graduated, whose chances were probably 500,000 to one than he would not make it. He had spent two years in the streets of Chicago. His mother had to make a choice between him and her boyfriend and she picked the boyfriend. He is now in college. Nobody gave him a chance. Now that's a real success story."

"We had a student who was really struggling. We got him involved with an agency that found him a place to stay. What really made it successful was that the clerks in the office took him under their wing and really got him to come in and work during his free period and lunch period. Got him answering phones and working in the office and they just fawned all over him and made him feel very, very good and very special. Helped get him through the bad times. Now he's on the honor roll even though he's on his own in life. Things like this really make it worthwhile."

"I had a young man in our alternative program. He was incarcerated and during that time we would correspond, we would write back and forth. In his letters he would reflect. I remember, he would write, you told me such and such and that if I would work hard I could do it and that I had a good heart. When he was released for good behavior he called me the next day. To me that was a success."

"We had a young lady who started in kindergarten seven years ago. Wheelchair-bound and unable to move except to have her eyes go up and down. At that time she was not expected to live beyond the fifth grade. Well she not only lived, but she continued. She came to school initially just for a couple of hours a day because that was all she could handle. Eventually as the years went on, she increased her time at school. She insisted in her own way because we learned how to communicate with her. One of my biggest thrills was last year when she was a sixth-grader and moved on to our middle school. And to think that a youngster with so many needs, whose assistant nurse was with her all the time, to see how those youngsters who went through school with her have grown in terms of their capacity to care, their capacity to be sensitive to all kinds of people as a result. She gave far more than any of us could possibly have given to her."

"At the beginning of the second semester three years ago one of our seniors was diagnosed with a brain tumor. He went from walking and being involved with everybody to being in a wheelchair quickly. We didn't know if he would make it to Easter. He was going to be the first in his family to graduate from high school. We got a home-bound teacher to work with his teachers to determine what he needed to do to earn a diploma. We went to the senior class and we met each of the students in the beginning of the week that we decided to have him graduate. We told them we were going to be celebrating his graduation early on Sunday. We had seven hundred seats in the auditorium and it was basically filled for his separate graduate ceremony. The teachers and students pulled together and showed up to make this a celebration for him and his family."

Effective principals find much about their jobs to be rewarding. Primarily this revolves around performance of others, especially students. They make great investments in their students and are joyful about the positive results of these investments. These successes make the long days and problems and stresses of the job more than worthwhile.

9

CAN YOU FIND AN EFFECTIVE PRINCIPAL FOR YOUR SCHOOL?

Can every principal become an effective principal? Unfortunately, no. Although there are many good principals in our schools, only a few are like the exceptional principals we have called effective principals. Are effective principals born or made? Probably both. Certainly they have learned much along the road from their experience, mentors, exemplars, and professional education that is important to how they work. But their success is also due to their personal qualities, both inborn and resulting from their upbringing.

Can every principal learn from effective principals? Fortunately, yes. There is much that principals can learn about how to make the use of a school mission or vision effective, how to move the school forward through celebrating, and how to work successfully with staff and students as individuals. They can learn to make better use of their time and to provide more integrity and unity to their work. The study of how effective principals work should be of value to any principal or principal in preparation. To learn to incorporate more of the effective principal's work style into one's work would probably proceed best with the assistance of a mentor. The mentor could help the principal assess her current activities, responses, and tendencies and monitor attempts to change them in the noble principal's direction.

EFFECTIVE PRINCIPALS APPLY POSITIVE PSYCHOLOGY

When we started this study we did not anticipate being able to describe the work of outstanding principals by using the basic principals of positive psychology. Clearly, however, that can be done. They way they work is overwhelmingly positive. Certainly anyone who is involved in the number of interactions and situations that the principal is cannot be positive in every case, but it is the positive character of the effective principal that stands out.

They have a concept of what the "good school" is that truly directs their work. For them the mission statement or vision is an article of faith by which they live. This contrasts sharply with the more common situation in which the school's mission statement is developed and then quickly set aside.

They understand the importance of building on success. Their extraordinary emphasis on celebration is one expression of this understanding. In every school there is celebration. Most schools, however, generally celebrate successful behaviors only in certain areas. It is done in a way that only the behavior of some can be celebrated. Celebration is used as a reward and to make some stand out. In the effective principal's school, however, celebration is designed to teach and reinforce those behaviors which are being sought. Effective principals use celebration to reward growth toward desired performance. In a sense this is a whole new concept of celebration than that found in most educational institutions where only top performers are celebrated. Celebration in the effective principal's school is part of the learning process.

These principals also use celebration to create a positive work climate for all. The power of such a climate cannot be overstated. When students and staff feel that they belong, they are able to dedicate their energies to learn and improve rather than to try to find acceptance. A positive work climate is contagious. It leads to success that leads to success.

Effective principals understand the importance of building people. Certainly education is a process of eliminating weaknesses as well as learning new things. As educators we have often been taught to correct, to focus on what is wrong. Effective principals have a different mindset. They focus on what the person can do and use that as a means to get them to do more. Many years ago we saw an article titled "Catch the child doing good." Effective principals operate from this perspective rather than a correcting one. Furthermore, they understand the importance of getting to know people well—staff or students—and earning their trust as a prerequisite to being able to help them, and they are willing to spend their time in so doing.

Effective principals are not defensive. This allows them to focus on others. They get their reinforcement from investing in others. They gain real strength from this. One of the co-authors of this study has for many years talked about the idea of the "dipper and the bucket." If you dip from your bucket of strength and pass it along to others you will find that there is now more in your own bucket, not less. This is the way it seems to work for these principals.

Effective principals understand that acting your way into good beliefs is the best way to create them. They focus on behavior and how to structure the situation so that good behavior will occur. This is why they take the time to have kindergarten students sing the school song, as is done at Wyoming school. It gets the students to voice the behaviors to achieve. This is why principals construct activities such as one we saw in an elementary school. The students were returning from recess. Two students were selected to hold the doors open for the others. Each entering student thanked the door holders, who responded to each with "You're welcome." Practicing good behavior in a positive environment creates good behavior.

Similarly all principals can practice the behaviors of effective principals to become more effective themselves. It is not easy for the principal to develop new behaviors, however, because they are so incredibly busy that there is not much time for deliberate planning and reflection. This is why we suggest that a mentor will be needed.

RECRUITING HIGHLY ABLE INDIVIDUALS TO THE PRINCIPALSHIP

There is considerable concern today that the "pipeline" of highly able people preparing to be principals is not very full. The principals in this study frequently voiced this. All too often teachers who might be good prospects for the principalship are deciding that the demands of the job are too much and are staying put in the classroom. Almost half the schools responding to a survey conducted by the National Association of Elementary School Principals and the National Association of Secondary School Principals reported a shortage of qualified candidates for their principal positions.[1] The financial rewards of the job are no longer enough to attract talented teachers to leave the classroom to become principals as they once did.

Most of the principals in this study became principals due to one or more of these reasons:

- They were influenced by a mentor who guided them to the position.
- They had a desire to have a broader influence in the school than one can have as a classroom teacher.
- They believed they could do a better job than principals they had observed or for whom they had worked.

Perhaps these give us some direction for spotting people to become principals.

All who are concerned about the quality of schools in this country must be recruiters for the principalship. We need to encourage able individuals in the direction of this career. It's not too early to focus on high school students who appear to have the right kind of leadership qualities. Just as many people think it is right to encourage outstanding secondary school students to prepare to be doctors or engineers, we should encourage them to consider being principals as well. Teachers and principals can spot students in their schools with the personal characteristics essential to become effective principals. They should not hesitate to talk with such students about this career. Furthermore they should seek to provide them leadership and other opportunities to learn about the work of the principal. For example, the school could have some kind of student intern principal position to develop interest in the work. Principals can be effective recruiters by enabling students in their schools to learn more about the rewards of their job.

Teachers are, of course, the primary prospects for people to prepare to be principals. Certainly principals must be on the lookout for teachers who are good candidates for the principalship.

"To get a promising teacher thinking about being a principal you have to tell them they should consider it. There have been some teachers that as early as their first year of teaching I could see that they had the capacity, they had the desire and the energy to do it. People who can keep many balls in the air at the same time, that can multitask and find interest in lots of different things. At first they have said 'no, no' to my suggestion that they should consider becoming principals. Then you need to provide them opportunities that show them how much fun this work can be; get them involved. If you have the right person, you can soon see the excitement building within her because she, too, will see the potential."

Schools should consider setting up formal mentoring programs to acquaint teachers with the work of the principal. This might be done by having some kind of intern position that a different teacher holds each year. Or it might be a multiyear plan to prepare a specific individual for the principalship. This could include serving as an assistant principal. In large schools, sometimes the role of the assistant principal can be quite narrow (e.g., discipline, athletic director), so if someone is being groomed to become a principal they should not stay in such an assignment very long. Perhaps equally as valuable as being an assistant principal can be committee work and other responsibilities where the individual has the opportunity to exercise leadership, work with community and parent groups, and work with people and in areas that are new for her.

If there is to be an adequate supply of principals to meet the needs of tomorrow's schools it is essential that current principals give attention to programs to provide students and teachers a chance to learn about the job and its rewards.

SEARCHING FOR A NEW PRINCIPAL

Perhaps the ideal situation is when there is a person within the school who is fully prepared to step into the principalship when it is vacant. That certainly makes finding the new principal relatively easy. There are circumstances, however, when it is best to go outside to find the new principal. Obviously there may not be a strong candidate within the school system or there may be a need for a break with the current leadership direction of the school. In this situation all those who will be involved in the hiring process—the school board, superintendent, and others—need to conduct a very active search to find their next principal. In years past it was sufficient to advertise the position and wait for candidates to apply. Today, that will most likely not produce a top principal for the job. Today it is a recruitment process. To find the right person for the job it is necessary to work hard to find strong candidates and to put out the proverbial red carpet to let them know how much they are wanted.

Contacts can be made with universities preparing principals to get their recommendations for outstanding principals. Similarly professional associations of school administrators can be contacted. Ask respected school leaders for their recommendations of who the best principals are and who should be recruited for your position. From these kinds of sources those seeking a new principal can prepare a list of the top prospects in their region.

After you have prepared your list of top prospects, contact them personally. Perhaps a letter for introductory purposes is needed but a personal contact is a must to convey to these individuals your desire to find the best possible principal for your school. They will become excited about your job only if you can convey your excitement about it to them. A personal contact is also the best way to learn more about the potential candidate.

When candidates come to your school for an interview it is important to remember that you are both selecting and selling. You want to observe the candidate interacting with many people and in many situations. The schedule should allow for the candidate to do things as well as talk about them (e.g., visit classes and be part of the learning activity, meet students in the halls, be part of a teacher discussion group). But you also want to focus on showing her what is great about your school and to emphasize how her skills will meet the needs of the school.

KEEPING THE PRINCIPAL

There is a line in the musical *South Pacific* that states, "Once you have found him, never let him go." That's a good directive to you when you are successful in hiring an outstanding principal for your school. Obviously you have asked that person to take on a challenging and demanding job. When she receives support from the community and within the school system, she will be stronger in her work. And she will stay on the job longer.

Fortunately, principals tend not to be job hoppers but to stay and make an investment in their position. A recent study in our state (Nebraska) noted that the average time a principal had served in that position was about nine years. In that study those who moved from one principalship to another did so primarily to earn a higher salary or to get a higher level of community support. These are situations that their original school district often could meet if it so desired. Most principals view their job as a career. They are not passing through the principalship on their way to something else. A 1998 survey by the National Association of Elementary School Principals revealed that less than 1 percent of the principals surveyed reported that their morale was bad.[2] Almost nine out of ten indicated that if they were to start all over again that they would choose to be principals.

Top principals are learners. They see each situation as an opportunity to learn. Because of this they readily adjust to the new circumstances they encounter. They work to build the community necessary to have a successful organization. These qualities are among those that enable them to be effective in a position over a period of years.

Whether it is by the board of education, the superintendent, teachers individually and collectively, or whomever, it is important that thought be given to how to support and applaud the principal. Certainly this must be tailored to the personality of the principal. Everyone benefits from some form of recognition for what they are doing well. For some an event like a "former student week" will be very rewarding. For some personal comments of appreciation and praise will be important. Recognition of the commitment that the principal makes to the school can come from many different sources. It's a tough job. Expressions of appreciation and concern, no matter how delivered, can help the principal maintain the high level of activity and commitment expected of her.

Another crucial aspect of supporting the principal is to give her the authority necessary to do the job. Even though great principals do not behave in an autocratic manner they must have power to get their jobs done. If that power is undercut by the various communities with whom they work or by their superiors they will not be successful.

Research on for-profit organizations has revealed that organizations that provide their leaders and managers with strong positive and legitimate authority are more likely to be successful. When leaders are supported they can more confidently create the conditions that will promote positive performance by the employees of the organization. Providing the leader a supportive environment helps her to grow and thus be a more effective leader for those with whom she works. Positive leaders produce more engaged employees, who produce more effective organizations.

The results of finding and keeping a top principal, most especially what we have called an effective principal, for your school will be more than worth the effort of so doing. The effective principal will produce a positive school environment that will help teachers do their best work. This environment will support student learning and will give all students a real shot at success in school. What better outcomes could we seek?

CLOSING THOUGHTS

Effective principals are a special breed of people. They find their success in the success of those with whom they work and continue to believe in them no matter how rough the journey. For them their work is a calling. For them their work is an end in itself. They derive personal fulfillment from what they view as meaningful work that makes the world a better place. They draw strength from doing their work. They invest in their schools. They persist.

We all owe them a great debt of gratitude for the leadership they provide. The principalship truly is a noble profession.

NOTE

1. Educational Research Service, National Association of Elementary School Principals, and National Association of Secondary School Principals, "Is There a Shortage of Qualified Candidates for Openings in the Principalship? An Exploratory Study." (Arlington, VA: Educational Research Services, 1998).

2. Educational Research Service, National Association of Elementary School Principals, and National Association of Secondary School Principals, "The Principal, Keystone of a High-Achieving School: Attracting and Keeping the Leaders We Need." (Arlington, VA: Educational Research Services, 2000).

ABOUT THE AUTHORS

James O'Hanlon served as dean of Teachers College at the University of Nebraska–Lincoln from 1982 to 2003. He has leadership experience in schools, athletics, government, business, and the military.

Donald O. Clifton served as chairman of the Gallup Organization from 1969 to 2000. In 2000, he became chairman of the Gallup International Research and Education Center.

LaVergne, TN USA
15 March 2011
220133LV00005B/11/P